GW01373079

I SO
1 3 0882363 3

Art copyright © Hergé/Moulinsart 2007
Text copyright © Michael Farr 2007

The Adventures of Tintin have originally been translated into English
by Leslie Lonsdale-Cooper and Michael Turner
Copyright English translation of the balloons by Egmont Books

Every effort has been made to contact the holders of all copyright material reproduced
in this book. In the event that any have been inadvertently overlooked, representation
should be made to Éditions Moulinsart, 162 avenue Louise, 1050 Bruxelles, Belgium,
who will be pleased to rectify the situation at the earliest opportunity.

First published in Great Britain in 2007 by John Murray (Publishers)
An Hachette Livre UK company

1

The right of Michael Farr to be identified as the Author of the Work has been asserted
by him in accordance with the Copyright, Designs and Patents Act 1988

All rights reserved. No part of this publication may be reproduced, stored in a retrieval system,
or transmitted, in any form or by any means without the prior written permission of the publisher,
nor be otherwise circulated in any form of binding or cover other than that in which it is published
and without a similar condition being imposed on the subsequent purchaser.

A CIP catalogue record for this title is available from the British Library

ISBN 978-0-7195-6799-5

Printed and bound in Belgium

John Murray (Publishers)
338 Euston Road
London NW1 3BH
www.johnmurray.co.uk

MICHAEL FARR

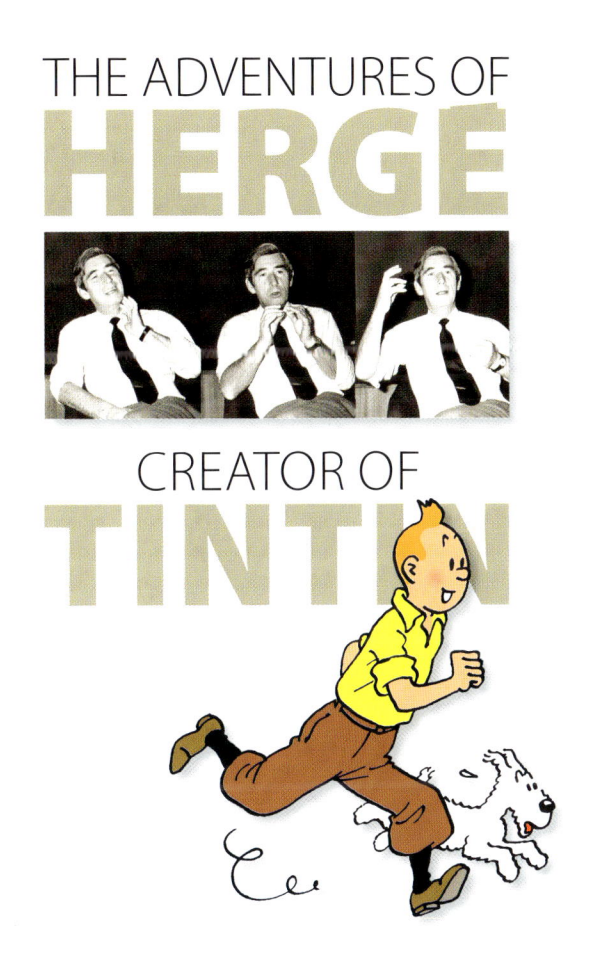

THE ADVENTURES OF
HERGÉ

CREATOR OF
TINTIN

Somerset Library Service	
1 3 0882363 3	
Askews	30-Oct-2007
741.509	£20.00

JOHN MURRAY

Acknowledgements

First and foremost I must thank Fanny Rodwell for talking to me about her life with Hergé whom she first met in 1955, lived with from 1960 and married in 1977. Nobody can have a better understanding of his complex and endearing personality. To have gone through the photographs they took together and to have spent time in the home they shared, surrounded by the art he loved, the books he read, the records they listened to, conjured up an almost intimate picture of a very private man.

I am most grateful to Guy and Léona Dessicy, whose friendship with Hergé dates back to the 1930s, for their insights into his character, intense sense of loyalty and, above all, humour. Guy Dessicy, who worked with Hergé from 1947 to 1953 and was an original member of the Studios in 1950 before he left to establish the Publiart advertising agency, provided a wealth of detail about Hergé the man and artist. That, for instance, he found it remarkably hard to draw the Thom(p)sons' bowler hats and also the telephones that feature so often in the adventures.

I am also indebted to Raymond Leblanc who on the day of Hergé's centenary on 22 May 2007 celebrated his own 92nd birthday, having the previous year had a Brussels foundation named after him. An Anglophile with a love of lawn tennis and equestrianism, it was the war hero Leblanc who brought Hergé back into journalism by founding *Tintin* magazine in September 1946, and so ensuring the continuation of Tintin's adventures. Apart from his reminiscences about Hergé, I shall always remember the excellence of the claret he had served at lunch, the equal of the marvellous Burgundy I remember drinking with Hergé almost 30 years previously.

I must also thank another nonagenarian Tintinophile, Stefanie Jordan, for her help on this and previous books and notably the information she was able to give about Hergé's brother Paul – the model for Tintin – whom she got to know after the war when he was appointed Belgian commandant in Bad Godesberg, near Bonn, and who used to go out riding every morning with her husband Colonel Jack Jordan.

Étienne Pollet provided a wealth of information about Hergé and his relationship with the publisher Casterman, whose best-selling author he became after the war. Charles Dierick, who has made a study of Hergé and the cinema, was very helpful offering material on the influence of films in his work. Ivan Noerdinger deserves a special credit for inspiring the start of the book, Dominique Maricq for culling fascinating illustrations from the archives, Michel Bareau for his cover that distils graphically its essence, and particularly Catherine Thirry for her inspired and elegant artistic design. The book could not have been written without the help and encouragement of Mark Rodwell and most importantly its instigator, Didier Platteau, head of publishing at Moulinsart, and latterly Régine Vandamme. At John Murray I would like to give special thanks to Roland Philipps, Caroline Westmore and Lucy Dixon. ∎

4
INTRODUCTION

7
KEY DATES IN THE LIFE OF HERGÉ

8
THE DEATH OF AN ARTIST

24
A PASSION FOR ART

42
A JOURNALIST AT HEART

58
THE LURE OF THE SILVER SCREEN

74
BE PREPARED! A LIFELONG BOY SCOUT

88
ORIENTAL ATTRACTION

108
AN ELEGANT JOKER, WITH A SERIOUS SIDE

126
INDEX

Introduction

Georges Remi, known worldwide as Hergé, was an extremely private man responsible for creating a very public figure – Tintin. Originally intended in 1929 for the entertainment and education of young Belgians, the quiff-haired reporter with the then highly fashionable plus fours, became an almost instant phenomenon in the French-speaking world. Tintin was a hero, even in Francophone Africa, where, oblivious of modern perceptions of 'political correctness', the flawed but entertaining *Tintin in the Congo* (1931) quickly became a favourite adventure.

Although, like Hergé, distinctly Belgian and Bruxellois in origin, the remarkable reporter was adopted by the French as their own by 1930, appearing in the children's publication *Cœurs Vaillants*. Some thirty years later French president Charles de Gaulle could declare memorably and immodestly that Tintin was his 'only international rival.' Switzerland, a country for which Hergé was to develop a special affection and which was to be his refuge at times of difficulty and depression, was Tintin's next conquest where his adventures began to appear as early as 1932 in *L'Écho Illustré*. One of Hergé's ideas of bliss was to sit on a terrace by lake Geneva eating *filets de perche* (perch fillets) and sipping the local *vin du Valais*, which on one occasion he helped to harvest and which Captain Haddock thirsts for in a tantalising sequence in *The Calculus Affair*.

Portugal followed in 1936 in the children's magazine *O Papagaio*, marking the first translation of the reporter's adventures from French. Even before Tintin became known there, Hergé had created a delightful character, the inestimable merchant Senhor Oliveira da Figueira from Lisbon in *Cigars of the Pharaoh* (1932–3), demonstrating his affection for the Portuguese. On his introduction in the first black-and-white version, Snowy remarks: 'A Portuguese? The Portuguese are always fun!…' During the difficult war years he was able to order – against his royalties – food parcels, filled with tins of sardines, cured sausages and other delicacies, from his publisher in neutral Lisbon for himself in German-occupied Brussels, where food supplies were short, and passed on by the Red Cross for his brother, languishing in a prisoner-of-war camp in Germany. One 18-kilo package sent to Brussels in mid 1943 contained 45 tins of sardines, 10 packets of almonds and six bags of figs!

After the Second World War Tintin became known to Dutch readers as Kuifje, and during the 1950s he was introduced successfully to audiences in Britain, Germany and Spain. In Britain the waters were first tested in *Eagle* comic before the adventures, one by one and out of sequence, were taken up by Methuen Children's Books, encouraged by a timely and highly favourable review in the *Times Literary Supplement*. The rest of the world followed and by the time of the celebrations of Hergé's centenary in 2007, the tally for *The Adventures of Tintin* had risen to a total of altogether over 200 million copies sold in some 70 languages.

In his lifetime Hergé, a man of natural modesty, was staggered and, of course delighted, by the success of Tintin, partly modelled on his younger brother Paul and partly on himself. 'I transposed my own thirst for adventures, so Tintin was me with everything in me that needed to be heroic, courageous, upright…' he wrote to his close friend Marcel Dehaye in July 1948. However, the popularity of Tintin increasingly became a tyranny, for, ignoring his own urge for respite and change, Hergé's public demanded a constant stream of new adventures. As author and artist, Hergé was meticulous in his approach and the pressure to produce was at times too much for him, causing him to erupt in boils and bringing him to the brink of nervous breakdown. As the years advanced the intervals between Tintin adventures lengthened despite the assistance from 1950 onwards of the Studios Hergé, set up to share some of the more labour-intensive work: colouring, inking, secondary details, etc. The demands of Tintin were exhausting, especially in Hergé's last years as his energy was increasingly sapped by the leukaemia that was to strike him down. Having stipulated that *The Adventures of Tintin* could not be continued by anyone else after his death – since he identified so closely with the principal characters – he would have been astonished at the steady subsequent advance of Tintin, as he continues to be discovered in new countries, more even than the redoubtable reporter managed to travel to. Following his death there were some at the Studios who felt that without new adventures interest in Tintin was bound to fade. They underestimated the enduring appeal of the intrepid reporter, however.

Hergé had a lifelong fascination for the world around him and all that was new. This did not mellow with age; his curiosity persisted to the end. He himself considered his principal characteristic to be 'curiosity allied to perfectionism.' As a Boy Scout he had appropriately been given the name 'Curious Fox.' Tintin reflected two of Hergé's predominant interests: art and news. For this reason, the Tintin books mirror in a remarkable way both the latest developments in modern art and world events in the twentieth century. A surprising awareness of avant-garde art is evident already in the first adventure *Tintin in the Land of the Soviets* (1929–30). Then 'in 1938 I had the Miró shock,' according to his own account, from which stemmed his overriding love of abstract art, a passion he had the time to cultivate from the 1960s onwards, encouraged by his friendship with the dealer Marcel Stal. He put down his thoughts: 'I think it is easier to dream or meditate in front of an abstract painting than a figurative one: the figurative painting imposes on the viewer its subject matter and therefore its limits, whereas an abstract painting leaves him his freedom. Moreover, abstract art requires greater participation on the spectator's part. It is also an art form which penetrates into the subject. For centuries, artists saw things from a distance; then came the Impressionists, who broke down light, the Cubists, who broke down the object, and with abstract art, matter itself was broken down… On the one hand, reality is very important to me. But on the other, I enjoy dreaming in front of an abstract piece of art, exactly as one can dream while gazing at clouds.'

Hergé would have been highly amused to find that at the time of his centenary the premises of Marcel Stal's Carrefour gallery at 170 Avenue Louise – a few doors along from the Studios Hergé at 162 – which he initially helped finance and to which he would adjourn daily at midday for 'an aperitif and art' had become a ladies' hairdresser and beautician with the name 'Zen Coiffure.' Hergé had a profound interest in Zen Buddhism that, according to Fanny, his wife at the time, he could link to his love of abstract art.

As an art collector he was always exploring new directions and his list of acquisitions was long. It included works by his hero Joan Miró, Sonia Delaunay, Jean Dubuffet, Auguste Herbin, Pierre Alechinsky, Lucio Fontana, Serge Poliakoff, Frank Stella, Dan Flavin, Victor Vasarely, Karel Appel, Kenneth Noland, Robert Rauschenberg, Andy Warhol and Roy Lichtenstein. On one of his London visits he acquired a work, 'White Spring' by Richard Lin from Marlborough Fine Art in Old Bond Street and, according to Marcel Stal, he was interested in acquiring a painting by David Hockney. Although quite happy in Brussels – apart from a moment of deep disillusionment immediately after the war when he briefly toyed with the idea of emigrating to South America – he later declared London and Rome to be the cities he would most like to live in. When in New York he bought a cut-out nude (1970) by Tom Wesselman from the Sidney Janis Gallery. He made his last acquisitions from his hospital bed: two works by Stefan DeJaeger each entitled *Bleu de Nuit*, dated 1982, and made up of photographs on wooden panels arranged to show a silhouette in movement. Strongly reminiscent of Hergé's own work in subject and representation – the profile even resembles him – they mark a fitting epilogue to his collecting days.

Now with the acquisition in 2007 by the Centre Pompidou in Paris of a page of his drawings for *The Calculus Affair* for its permanent collection of modern art, Hergé has himself joined the pantheon of artists to be found in museums and his work can hang alongside the modern painters he loved so much, an accolade he would with his incorruptible modesty never have contemplated.

Time too will soon bring to fruition his hope – expressed months before his death – that Steven Spielberg, whose early films he admired greatly, would bring his characters to life on the screen. 'I believe that my way of telling a story comes much nearer to that of ordinary cinema than that of animated drawings,' he stated. Writing as early as June 1939 for his old school magazine, the Saint-Boniface Review, he said he saw things 'as in the cinema' – the techniques, cutting, long-shots, close-ups, etc.

Gradually, as the years pass, the veil is being lifted on an artist who despite the ever-spiralling success of Tintin preferred his life to be out of the limelight, to be shrouded in secrecy, even mystery. Like Tintin himself, his origins were largely kept under wraps. We know that his father and uncle were twins born scandalously to an unmarried chambermaid employed at a house belonging to a widowed countess*, that they were well provided for and that a suitable artisan husband, called Remi and ten years her junior, was in due course found for the single mother. Hergé mischievously encouraged speculation on the possible pedigree of his grandfather. Could it have been the king (Léopold II) himself? No such evidence has ever materialised and the most likely explanation seems to be that the twins resulted from an amorous liaison between the chambermaid and an aristocratic house-guest, or, more prosaically, may have followed an altogether more commonplace union.

Hergé, incidentally, was an avid royalist and made sure that Léopold III and his family received signed and dedicated copies of each Tintin adventure on publication from 1930 onwards. An exhibition at the Royal Palace in Brussels on the occasion of Hergé's centenary displayed the Tintin first editions with the author's royal dedications. The king was as enthusiastic about Tintin as his subjects. Hergé delighted in his encounter with Léopold during the former king's post-war exile in Switzerland and their joint fishing trips on Lake Geneva.

There is also a certain amount of fog regarding Hergé's mother Élisabeth, a striking beauty in her youth who became mentally unstable and ended her life in an asylum. She was distraught at the capture and imprisonment of her younger, soldier son Paul during the war and when she saw a newspaper notice of the death of a similarly named officer she believed it to be him. When following his liberation in April 1945, Paul, accompanied by his brother Georges, first visited her, she refused to believe it was really her son. Hergé had a lifelong fear of madness and the possibility that he might inherit his mother's mental illness. This makes the frequent allusions to and instances of madness in *The Adventures of Tintin* particularly personal, poignant and disquieting.

In this biographical portrait I have taken seven key aspects of his life, perhaps appropriate for someone born in the seventh year of the century who relished the positive associations of the number, and in sketching them have attempted to give a picture of the complex and remarkable man who left in Tintin a legacy of such universal appeal. Understanding Hergé helps us to fathom the phenomenal success of the heroic boy reporter he created and may enhance our enjoyment of his adventures further. ∎

Michael Farr

---

* The Countess Marie-Hélène de Dudzeele.

KEY DATES IN THE LIFE OF HERGÉ

1907, 22 May Born Georges Remi in the Etterbeek district of Brussels. His father, Alexis, has an identical twin Léon, providing future inspiration for the creation of the bungling detectives Thomson and Thompson. His mother, Élisabeth, shows signs of the mental illness she will later develop. Madness becomes a recurrent theme in *The Adventures of Tintin*.

1924 Georges Remi devises the pen name Hergé, resulting from the reversal of his initials, as pronounced in French.

1925 Gains his first employment after leaving school, working in the subscriptions department of the Catholic newspaper *Le Vingtième Siècle*.

1926 Creates a comic strip with the Boy Scout patrol leader Totor, the precursor of Tintin, for the scouting magazine *Le Boy-Scout Belge*.

1928 Having provided illustrations for various parts of *Le Vingtième Siècle*, he is put in charge of a newly created children's supplement, *Le Petit Vingtième*.

1929, 10 January Introduces Tintin (and Snowy – or Milou in French, after his first girlfriend) to the pages of *Le Petit Vingtième*. The fledgling reporter gains instant popularity.

1930, 23 January Introduces the two Brussels scallywags, Quick and Flupke, to *Le Petit Vingtième*.

1932 After a long courtship marries Germaine Kieckens, the secretary of Father Norbert Wallez, the director of *Le Vingtième Siècle*, at Laeken on the outskirts of Brussels.

1934 Meets and befriends the Chinese art student Chang Chong-chen, also aged 27, who explains to him the finer points of Eastern art, poetry and philosophy and gives him an understanding of the orient and openness to other cultures that he is never to lose. The result is *The Blue Lotus*, his first masterpiece, which marks a qualitative departure from the more naive, though successful, earlier adventures in the Soviet Union, Congo and America. The long-established Tournai-based publisher Casterman takes over publication of the Tintin books.

1935 Creates the characters Jo, Zette and Jocko – a brother, sister and their pet chimpanzee – for the French children's weekly *Cœurs Vaillants* that wanted a more family-orientated series of adventures. The father is a civil engineer, the mother a housewife.

1938 Hergé is bowled over by the work of the Spanish surrealist painter Joan Miró who becomes his favourite modern artist. Botticelli remains his preferred old master.

1940, May Germany invades Belgium and for the second time in his life Hergé experiences the German occupation of Brussels. The Catholic *Le Vingtième Siècle* closes down but Tintin quickly moves to Belgium's leading daily, *Le Soir*, which creates a special weekly supplement for the reporter, *Le Soir Jeunesse*. Unfortunately, realising the importance of *Le Soir*, the occupying authorities take control of it and compromise both Tintin and Hergé. The first use of colour in the Tintin strips.

1942 At Casterman's request, Hergé begins to recast the existing Tintin adventures into a standard 62-page book format and puts them into full colour.

1946 His mother Élisabeth dies in a mental hospital. He continues to be barred from journalism because of his wartime association with *Le Soir* until the entrepreneur and resistance hero Raymond Leblanc obtains for Hergé a 'good conduct certificate' clearing him of any wrongdoing. In September Leblanc launches the weekly *Tintin* magazine with Hergé as artistic director. The magazine has Tintin as its centrepiece and enjoys considerable success with a public eager to be distracted from post-war austerity.

1950 Hergé goes through a period of deep depression and for a period is unable to continue Tintin. Sets up the Studios to lighten the workload and embark on the two Moon books.

1953 Lands Tintin on the Moon in highly realistic circumstances sixteen years before Neil Armstrong's first step.

1956 Casterman's sales of the Tintin books reach the million mark. Hergé falls in love with Fanny Vlamynck, a 22-year-old colourist who had joined the Studios the previous year.

1960 Having weathered a personal crisis reflected in the making of *Tintin in Tibet*, an adventure about the overpowering strength of friendship, Hergé decides to make the break from his first marriage and set up home with Fanny. He begins to travel with her and cultivates his love of modern art.

1976 Publication of *Tintin and the Picaros*, the last completed adventure. To the disappointment of many readers, Tintin for the first time changes out of his plus fours into brown jeans.

1977 The divorce from his first wife, Germaine, is finally promulgated and in May he marries Fanny in Brussels.

1981 In March has an emotional reunion at Brussels airport with his old friend Chang who returns to Belgium for the first time since 1935. Together with his son spends three months with Hergé, by now visibly ailing.

1983 Hergé dies on 3 March after a long leukaemia-related illness, and is mourned throughout the world. ■

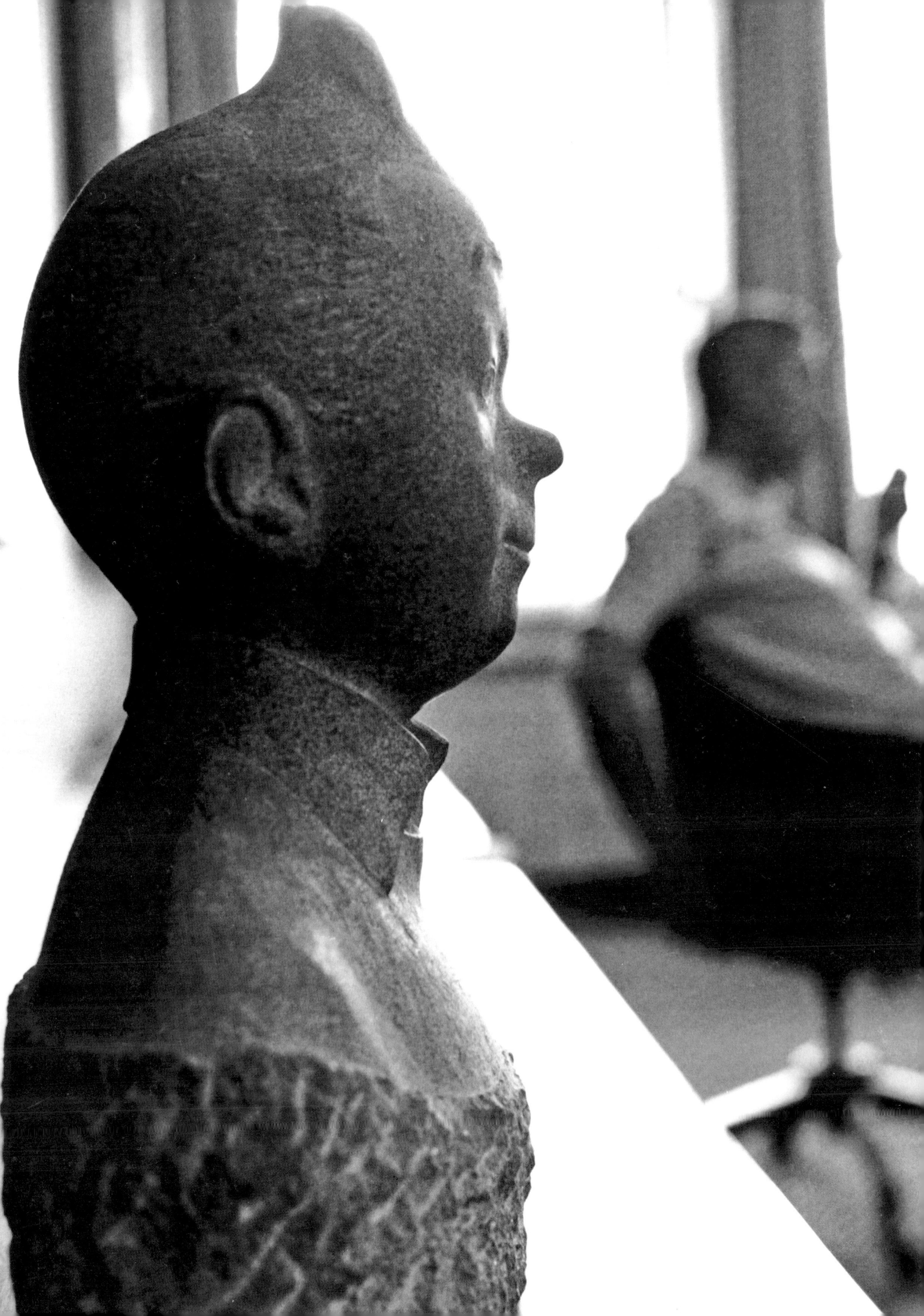

CHAPTER ONE
The death of an artist

March 1983 was a bleak month; the carnival festivities were over, Lent was under way. The month, during which two millennia earlier Julius Caesar had been brutally murdered in the Roman Forum, began with general elections in France and Germany, and the Polish Pope John Paul II, himself recently recovered from an assassination attempt two years earlier in Rome, touring a strife-torn Central America.

ANGUISH

Meanwhile, in Brussels, the bureaucratic heart of Europe, an ambulance had rushed Georges Remi to hospital on 25 February. The seventy-five-year-old – better known as Hergé, the creator of Tintin – was gravely ill. He had been for some time, chronically weakened by anaemia brought on by a leukaemia-like illness, osteomyelofibrosis to be precise. Now, battling with pneumonia, he had a cardiac arrest. In hospital, he pressed his wife Fanny's hand and said he loved her. He was wheeled into intensive care and slipped into a coma that caused the utmost concern. He had left Tintin in equally dire straits – about to be cast into a 'living statue' by his arch-enemy. This time there seemed to be little hope for either the author or the famous reporter.

In the final completed Tintin adventure, *Tintin and the Picaros*, published in 1976, Hergé had originally begun with the reporter arriving at Marlinspike by motorcycle across an invigorating early summer landscape, meadows aglow with flowers – poppies and blue cornflowers. When colleagues pointed out that the story was unfolding in February during carnival time, he had to revise the rural setting, stripping the trees of their verdant foliage and the fields of their crops to leave bare furrows. Hungry birds are silhouetted in flight, in the manner of the seventeenth-century Flemish artist Jacob van Ruisdael, whose work was familiar to Hergé, or perched expectantly on branches, providing the only sign of life as a leaden sky weighs down on the scene, just as it did during those early March days of 1983.

Amid this seasonal gloom, hope faded for Hergé and Tintin. Finally, on 3 March, towards 10 p.m., the Saint-Luc Clinic in Brussels confirmed his death. Although hardly surprising, like all deaths it was a shock, to his widow Fanny, his first wife Germaine and his many friends, as well as to an audience across the world which was to become even larger than he can have imagined. His immediate circle had lost a personality full of humour and sensitivity, while the world was deprived of an entertainer with an extraordinary universality of appeal.

LEFT PAGE
This time there seemed to be little hope for either the author or the famous reporter.

THE ADVENTURES OF HERGÉ, CREATOR OF TINTIN

4 F • SAMEDI 5 ET DIMANCHE 6 MARS 1983 • Nlle SÉRIE • N° 558

Libération

LA DERNIERE AVENTURE DE TINTIN

FRANCE, RFA VOTES EN STOCK

"WAAOOOUUU... TINTIN EST MORT.."

Algérie : 2,50DA • Belgique : 27F • Canada : $1,10 • Côte d'Ivoire : 430F CFA • Espagne : 110Ptas • Etats-Unis : $0,95 • Grèce : 60DR • Italie : 1200L • Luxembourg : 27F • Portugal : 60Esc • Sénégal : 400F CFA • Suisse : 1,70F • Tunisie : 380M

As an aspiring journalist and the creator of the world's best-known reporter, his departure was quickly reported, featuring on television and radio bulletins in his native Belgium, France and around the world, reminiscent of that memorable sequence in *The Blue Lotus*, perhaps his finest book, where the Radio Tokyo news bulletin of the staged attack on the Shanghai–Nanking railway is relayed on radio sets across the globe to listeners in Europe, America, India and Africa.

The press, which ever since the triumphant return of Tintin from his first adventure to the Soviet Union in 1930, had adopted the boy reporter as a talisman, had a field day, with extensive reports and tributes. Every other newspaper, however, was upstaged by the French daily *Libération*, which, with a daring and inspired editorial decision, gave over its whole front page to the circled and black-framed image of a prone Tintin with Snowy howling by his side: 'WAAOOOUUUU!! Tintin is dead…'

Below the masthead was the familiar logo of the juxtaposed heads of Tintin and Snowy (bone in mouth) and the label: 'The Final Adventure of Tintin'. The cover had the headline in French 'FRANCE, RFA VOTES EN STOCK', referring on the one hand to imminent general elections in France and the Federal Republic of Germany and on the other to the Tintin adventure *Coke en Stock* (*Red Sea Sharks* in the English edition). The drawing of Tintin and Snowy was taken from the episode in *Tintin in Tibet* where the reporter lies unconscious in the wake of an avalanche. Inside the newspaper every page was illustrated by a geographically or politically relevant image from a Tintin adventure. The Pope's visit to troubled Central America, for instance, was accompanied by a defiant Tintin standing before a military firing squad in his first South American adventure, *The Broken Ear*. The pastoral nature of the Pope's foreign travel was, meanwhile, underlined by a sequence showing Tintin with the benevolent priest at the mission station in *Tintin in the Congo*. The point was made convincingly that Tintin, who had spent fifty years reporting the current affairs of the twentieth century, could embrace all news. He was completely relevant to people's daily lives.

Other newspapers chose to make Hergé's death their lead story; *Le Matin de Paris* had the headline 'Adieu Tintin…' below a large illustration of a desperate Tintin and Captain Haddock trekking across the scorching desert, taken from *The Crab with the Golden Claws*. Only Snowy with an outsize camel bone gripped firmly in his jaws displays any optimism.

There were numerous references to Tintin becoming an orphan, some printing the plate from page 5 of *Tintin in Tibet* where Tintin and Snowy shed tears at the thought of Chang's death, a rare instance of the reporter in tears. It was an image used on the front page of *Le Soir*, the newspaper for which Hergé controversially worked during the war years, giving Tintin a much larger audience in Belgium and establishing his fame. 'The whole world bids farewell to Hergé,' ran its headline.

Le Quotidien de Paris noted in a headline that in Belgium Tintin was 'a national hero' and selected a number of characters from the books to offer invented quotes on the death of Hergé. Bianca Castafiore promises predictably: 'And now in his memory let me sing the Jewel Song from Faust…', a tribute which, like Haddock, he would sooner have been spared. But perhaps the most memorable observation came from the least significant character chosen, Mrs Piggott, the housekeeper of Professor Alembick at the start of *King Ottokar's Sceptre*. With great wisdom, she declares: 'And he was what's more a great draughtsman…'

TRIBUTES

News of Hergé's death: *Vendredi Samedi Dimanche*.

LEFT
Front page of *Libération*, 5–6 March 1983.

Wallez's confidence in his protégé was justified; the supplement was a runaway success, requiring a repeatedly increased print run and giving the parent newspaper a considerable circulation boost.

The priest who directed the Catholic newspaper *Le Vingtième Siècle*, Father Norbert Wallez, had a liking for the young Georges Remi and a strong belief in his ability.

A MASTER

Hergé was a wonderful storyteller, producing narratives of tremendous excitement and abundant humour, but he was also, despite all his modesty, a very significant draughtsman and artist. Mrs Piggott was right. As *L'Actualité* noted in another tribute, he was 'a master' and in Europe 'the father of the strip cartoon'. He was, furthermore, with *The Adventures of Tintin*, a conscientious chronicler of the turbulent twentieth century.

Like many self-taught artists, Hergé questioned his own talent. He knew what he could do and was highly aware of his limits. He had a passion for art that would never be fulfilled by his own ability. In his youth he walked out of a formal art class that he found too dull; late in life he tried his hand as an abstract painter but failed to convince himself or others that this was an avenue he should pursue. Yet he had a remarkable ability with pencil and pen and an acute sense of design. He was, in the words put into Mrs Piggott's mouth, truly a 'great draughtsman'.

TALENT FOR ADVERTISING, DESIGN

If he had not created Tintin he could have continued to devise arresting images and designs for advertising, as he did during the 1930s – book covers and typography as first commissioned by the publisher Casterman – or to draw for newspapers and magazines satirical caricatures that appealed to his delight in debunking the pompous and the all too serious. Yet his destiny was to raise the art of the strip cartoon, already defined in America, but fresh and full of possibilities in Europe. Tintin may have first emerged as a relatively spontaneous creation one day in January 1929, but this remarkable reporter was to evolve rapidly and develop into a durable artistic creation which earned the strip cartoon a new respectability and spawned a popular new form of art.

Hergé, however, remained surprised that something devised initially in fun to amuse children – and others as a bonus – should be taken so seriously. Art to him was something else, to be found in the paintings and sculptures of the artists he collected so avidly. His idea of art was something loftier. For that reason he was not particularly impressed by his success.

Recognition was quick in coming. Barely had Tintin come from his pen in those first tentatively defined images of the opening adventure, *Tintin in the Land of the Soviets*, than readers of the newly created *Le Petit Vingtième* supplement for children waited impatiently for the next week's issue. The priest who directed the Catholic newspaper *Le Vingtième Siècle*, Father Norbert Wallez, had a liking for the young Georges Remi and a strong belief in his ability. Recognising his talent for drawing, he promoted him from the subscriptions department where he was first employed. He could embellish the women's pages with elegant drawings of the latest fashions, or the book pages with suitable artwork, but best of all he could be put in charge of a new supplement for children. To fill some of this new space Hergé devised Tintin, a young journalist sent out to report some of the goings-on in the world featured in the main section of the newspaper. Wallez's confidence in his protégé was justified; the supplement was a runaway success, requiring a repeatedly increased print run and giving the parent newspaper a considerable circulation boost. While Tintin was wholly Hergé's creation, Wallez offered the platform for his launch and his extraordinary success.

Proof of Tintin's almost instant popularity came when Charles Lesne, a colleague of Hergé's on *Le Vingtième Siècle* who was later to become his key interlocutor at the publisher Casterman, suggested a stunt. Once the Soviet adventure had run its course in the pages of *Le Petit Vingtième*, a young man resembling Tintin should be found, along with an accompanying fox terrier, dressed 'à la Russe' and put on the train arriving in Brussels from Berlin and Moscow.

To fill some of this new space Hergé devised Tintin.

THE ADVENTURES OF HERGÉ, CREATOR OF TINTIN

A huge crowd flocked to the Gare du Nord to witness the spectacle.

A huge crowd flocked to the Gare du Nord to witness the spectacle. The Tintin who first appeared in print on 10 January 1929 had caught the public imagination to such an extent that people were prepared to applaud the return of his impersonation on 8 May 1930. A similar performance was enacted on 9 July 1931, to mark the end of Tintin's subsequent adventure in the Congo and his triumphant return to Brussels, this time in tropical gear complete with pith helmet and borne in a chair by African porters. Prior to the African voyage, Tintin and Snowy had gone to the Bon Marché department store in Brussels to be kitted out for the tropics, an episode paralleled by the budding reporter William Boot's visit to the emporium before his assignment to Ishmaelia in Evelyn Waugh's comic novel *Scoop* (1938). Boot and Tintin certainly compete in their inventory of excess and sometimes absurd baggage. Tintin's presence at Bon Marché was the reporter's first foray into advertising, something he would be able to pursue to Hergé's profit in years to come.

The first two adventures that had unfolded so successfully in the weekly pages of *Le Petit Vingtième* were, meanwhile, given permanence in book form, published by Father Wallez and Hergé under the imprint Les Éditions du Petit 'Vingtième'. By 1931 Tintin and Hergé were already well and truly established.

AN EXHAUSTING TRIUMPH

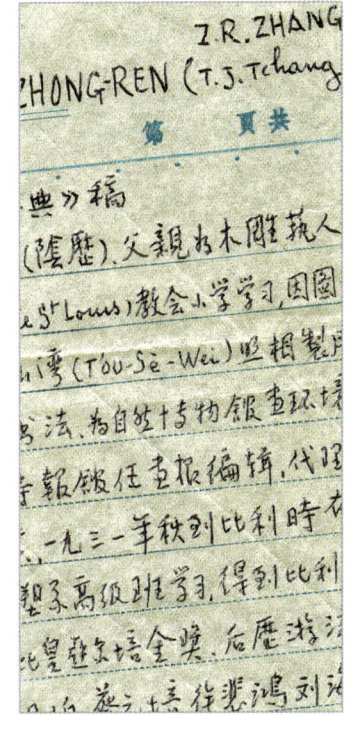

It was the elaborate fiftieth anniversary celebrations of Tintin's first appearance, laid on in an intensely proud Belgium in 1979, which really sapped Hergé's depleted reserves of energy, later to be boosted artificially by weekly blood transfusions. Tintin, if not Hergé, could claim 'most famous Belgian' status – despite attempts by the French to claim him as their own – and though they went against his modesty and hatred of any fuss, the author knew it would be churlish not to enter wholeheartedly into the festivities. Wherever he appeared he was questioned about where he was sending Tintin next. The last Tintin adventure, *Tintin and the Picaros*, had come out in 1976, and although a number of critics found it disappointing, readers were always eager and impatient for more. Hergé dropped clues about the new scenario; having toyed with the idea of setting an adventure at an airport, he was now working on a theme close to his heart: the world of art galleries, critics and forgeries. This was to be the unfinished *Tintin and Alph-Art*, published posthumously in sketch form.

Hergé's physical decline was visibly apparent by March 1981 when his long-lost but now rediscovered contemporary Chang was finally allowed to travel from Shanghai to Brussels for a moving reunion with the friend he had made during his student days in the Belgian capital. Despite the long journey and the unaccustomed media interest, Chang emerged as much more robust and youthful than Hergé – both men were born in 1907 – who found the whole proceedings a terrible strain, though overjoyed at the long-hoped-for meeting.

Hergé found increasingly that he had good days and bad ones when he lacked any energy. Gradually, as the months passed, the poor days began to gain dominance. It was no wonder that his work on the projected *Alph-Art* proceeded only fitfully. There would be a sudden flurry of activity on days when he felt better, sometimes fortified by a blood transfusion. He would joke that on these occasions he was going for a 'fill-up'.*

ALWAYS OPTIMISTIC

He thought of moving the studios in the Avenue Louise closer to his home, but time was running out. Tintin was waiting to be rescued. Hergé, optimistic by nature, thought he would pull through.

His optimism had been demonstrated by his long-held hope that one day he would re-establish contact with that very special friend he had made in 1934 and, sure enough, forty-seven years later, he was to embrace Chang again. It was the same with his favourite Siamese cat, Kang-Hi, which during the last year of his life unexpectedly went missing. The loss was deeply felt by Hergé and Fanny, for Kang-Hi had occupied a privileged position among the four household cats. As the days, weeks and months passed with no sign of the regal feline, Fanny came to accept the loss. But Hergé never gave up hope for the cat he considered 'as beautiful as a Chinese vase'.

So the man who with Snowy had created the most famous and popular dog of the strip cartoon, for the first time in his life acquired a dog – a whippet called Leila – to make up for the loss of his preferred Siamese. It was a hard gap to fill and the dog would look imploringly at her master, seeking but not really gaining the unqualified affection and approval she craved. The fact was that despite Snowy, Hergé was not, according to Fanny, so keen on dogs.

TOP
Chang travelled from Shanghai to Brussels for a moving reunion with the friend he had made during his student days.

ABOVE
Kang-Hi had occupied a privileged position among the four cats.

---

* He had gathered his ideas under the working title *A Winter's Day at an Airport – Un jour d'hiver, sur un aéroport*, which he planned as a rendezvous for a good number of characters from *The Adventures of Tintin*. Earlier *Flight 714* had got off to a promising start with its airport scenes, which were arguably more successful than the subsequent development of the story.

Nearly nine months later the telephone rang: Kang-Hi's collar and tag had been found in a garden many miles away from home, and there were reports of a Siamese cat scavenging among the dustbins behind a laundry. Fanny asked the caller to telephone at the next sighting, regardless of the hour. In due course the call came and Fanny and Hergé immediately set out by car, reached the destination and mounted watch from a garage near the dustbins. It was rather like a portside vigil by Tintin and Snowy, waiting and watching for the gangsters in one of the adventures. There was some movement by the bins. Fanny called out and the cat came; it was a very frightened and bedraggled Kang-Hi. In the back of the car on the journey home, the cat did not know which was more important – to guzzle the food on offer or, in cat fashion, to recount its adventures. Snowy too had on occasions been lost and, cold and hungry, had trekked great distances before being reunited with his master. Everybody was very happy – and Hergé especially, because yet again his optimism had proved justified and been rewarded. Once home, Kang-Hi immediately returned to the vacated position of authority, while the whippet had to accept its lot. Such were the differences and altercations between Snowy and the resident Siamese cat at Marlinspike.

Such were the differences and altercations between Snowy and the resident Siamese cat at Marlinspike.

It was one of the last adventures of Hergé's life as his strength ebbed away in the face of overpowering fatigue. The frequency of blood transfusions was increased to try to invigorate him but the benefits did not last. In his final months he was admitted to hospital twice.

The prospects may have been bleak but his optimism and humour prevailed, and there were occasional bright moments, as, for example, when he was photographed with the hospital staff, or learned with delight that his room looked on to the house where the widow of another notable twentieth-century Belgian artist, René Magritte, resided.

Fanny Rodwell has a wonderful photograph of him semi-recumbent, propped up on his pillows in his hospital bed with an appetising meal on the tray in front of him and a newly opened bottle of Bordeaux waiting to be enjoyed. Forty-two years earlier he had created Captain Haddock, the most popular character of *The Adventures of Tintin*, who enjoyed not only whisky but, like him, good wine. If Tintin himself reflected all the solid values Hergé had learned as a boy scout, then Haddock represented Hergé's other, more expansive side – his humanity and natural propensity to be a bon viveur. In the end, however, he remained 'more Tintin than Haddock', according to Fanny. None of his friends ever witnessed him drunk – never more than jolly – unlike the almost incorrigible captain. Only Professor Calculus's surreptitiously administered pills put Haddock off alcohol in *Tintin and the Picaros*, the final completed adventure.

AN ARMCHAIR TRAVELLER

One of the most curious aspects of the creator of Tintin was that until the autumn of his life Hergé hardly travelled. So while Tintin raced from Russia to the Congo, to the Americas North and South, Egypt, Arabia, India, China, Tibet and Indonesia, quite apart from western and central Europe and the ultimate destination, the Moon – sixteen years before the Americans landed on it – Hergé stayed at home. There were the early scouting trips to the Dolomites and the Pyrenees, and throughout his life he made a habit of visiting Switzerland, but essentially he was an armchair traveller par excellence. He would make up for the lack of his own air miles by disciplined and rigorous research, a careful compilation of documentation, which would ensure authenticity for Tintin's extensive travels. His own belated travels came too late to be of use for Tintin, but were nevertheless the source of great pleasure to the creator of the globe-trotting reporter.

CHAPTER ONE **THE DEATH OF AN ARTIST**

It was Hergé's relationship with and subsequent marriage to Fanny which prompted the delayed wanderlust. The years spent with his first wife Germaine had seen him tied to Belgium: Brussels and their country house at Céroux-Mousty in Brabant, supplemented only by the occasional escape to Switzerland. During the early 1950s, when he was near to a nervous breakdown and found he had to suspend work on Tintin, he would 'disappear' to Switzerland to be by himself.

It was with Fanny, however, that his horizons broadened and he began to travel frequently: at first short trips to Sicily – several times – Sardinia, Rome, Florence, Venice, Corsica; a less successful stay in Athens and Crete, Denmark and Sweden, and back to Switzerland for walking holidays – remembering his scouting days, he would insist on walking for six hours a day – and participation in the grape harvest, which delighted him. Then came the longer voyages, to the United States in 1971, initially to Chicago and to the Mayo Clinic in Minnesota for a medical consultation concerning liver problems. Relieved to be given the all-clear, and surprised at being prescribed something as simple as bicarbonate of soda for his distressed liver*, he and Fanny turned the trip into a long-overdue American tour.

From Chicago, where forty years earlier Tintin had busted Al Capone and the gangland syndicates and Hergé had caught the mood of this throbbing centre of modernism remarkably successfully, it was on to Kansas City, Los Angeles, Las Vegas and back to New York and Washington, from where they took the train to Miami. Additionally, time was found to visit the Oglala Sioux at their reservation at Pine Ridge, aided by a letter of introduction from the Indian enthusiast and expert, the Belgian priest Father Gall, an old contact of Hergé's.

ABOVE
Remembering his scouting days, he would insist on walking for six hours a day.

BELOW
It was with Fanny, however, that his horizons broadened and he began to travel frequently.

---

* 'I didn't need to travel thousands of kilometres to know that!' he joked afterwards. There had been concern that he might be suffering from cirrhosis of the liver.

TOP
When in New York Hergé visited Andy Warhol in his bizarrely peopled studio-workshop, the Factory. They were to meet again in Brussels, where Hergé showed Warhol his work.

ABOVE LEFT
Hergé improvising a placard at a congress of strip cartoonists, New York, 1972.

ABOVE RIGHT
The mayor of New York, John Lindsay, admiring Hergé's humorous poster of Tintin in the city.

NATIVE AMERICANS

Although he had described the exploitation of the Native Americans forthrightly and memorably in the scene where they are driven off their native lands at bayonet point by the National Guard so as to allow the oil tycoons to move in – one of the most powerful political statements in his œuvre – Hergé had always felt that he had not done justice to them in such early work as *Tintin in America*. He had portrayed them as being too naive, he believed later. For years afterwards he toyed with the idea of returning to the subject more thoroughly in a new adventure, but it was not to be. Meanwhile, together with Fanny, he had a number of meetings, including one with the grandson of the celebrated chief Red Cloud and also with Black Elk, an aged Native American who had been a guide at Mount Rushmore. They found the poverty and decline of a people who had until relatively recently been so free and proud a depressing experience, however.

In May of the following year, 1972, they returned to New York for a congress of strip cartoonists, for which Hergé improvised a placard showing a sequence in which Tintin, accompanied by Snowy, ambles down a street looking up, down, left and right until he crashes into a street sign and sees stars. The poster-size drawing is entitled 'Tintin Visiting New York… Or Stars and (Comic) Strip(e)s', with the reporter's still-stunned head superimposed on an American flag. He presented the sheet to the then mayor of the city, John Lindsay, with the inscription 'To New York City, with best wishes Hergé'.

When in New York Hergé visited Andy Warhol in his bizarrely peopled studio-workshop, the Factory. They were to meet again in Brussels, and Hergé was able to acquire three of a set of four portraits Warhol made of him. The sequence was put up in Hergé's office in the Avenue Louise opposite a set of screen prints by Roy Lichtenstein of Rouen cathedral, inspired by the paintings of Monet. Hergé tried unsuccessfully to see Lichtenstein during the New York visit. The two artists were admirers of each other's work, with the American producing a screen print of Tintin seated in his favourite red chair.

As on the previous American trip, Hergé and Fanny took in other destinations, including the Bahamas, where, on the idyllic Harbour Island, Hergé took pleasure in scuba diving. After so many years toiling over Tintin, meeting tight deadlines, leaving little time for himself, Hergé was developing a taste for travel and holidays which he took even further in 1973, the year he discovered Asia for himself – again some forty years after Tintin had sailed for the Orient.

Hergé with the grandson of the celebrated chief Red Cloud.

ASIA, AT LAST

Publication of *The Blue Lotus* (begun in 1934 in *Le Petit Vingtième*, appearing in 1936 in book form), with its graphic portrayal of naked Japanese aggression and imperialism, as well as the corruption of the International Settlement, solicited a formal complaint from the Japanese embassy to the Belgian Foreign Ministry.

There were also remonstrations from retired colonels and generals about the unsuitability and irrelevance of the subject to young Belgians. Its sensitivity to and sympathy for the Chinese cause won plaudits elsewhere including from China itself. As a result, in 1939 Hergé received an official invitation to visit the crisis-ridden country. With a world war looming, however, it was hardly the time for Hergé to start travelling, and the invitation from Madame Chiang Kai-shek, the wife of the Chinese nationalist leader, was put on ice. Internally riven and occupied by Japanese troops, China was to endure years of upheaval until the communists under Mao Zedong took control, driving the nationalists off the mainland and on to the island of Formosa (Taiwan).

Hergé and Fanny in Taiwan, 1973.

It was there finally – the invitation still standing – that Hergé travelled in 1973 for a fascinating taste of one side of China. He also went to Hong Kong and Macao and crossed to the New Territories, where he could peer over the British-patrolled frontier – perhaps remembering the International Settlement he had portrayed all those years earlier – at communist China itself. His hopes of going there later, particularly after he had received news of his old friend Chang, alive and despite everything surprisingly well in Shanghai, were to be undermined by that visit to Taiwan – his passport was embossed with the indelible visa stamp that the communists refused to acknowledge.

The Chinese experience was richly significant for Hergé, who ever since his meeting and friendship with Chang had steeped himself in Chinese philosophy and culture, particularly Taoism. His eyes had been opened to its wisdom, and he yearned for more.

During this year of travel he took in further Asian stops: Delhi on the way, enabling him to check the verisimilitude of his depiction of the city in *Tintin in Tibet* – in a delightful cameo Tintin and Haddock stop there too on their way to Kathmandu and Tibet – as well as additional holidays in Thailand and Bali in Indonesia. He had gathered a good deal of material on the Indonesian archipelago during the 1960s for *Flight 714*, which centres on the hijacking to one of the islands of a private jet bound for Sydney from Jakarta.

The final plate of the adventure has them resuming the journey and boarding Qantas Flight 714 to Sydney.

HAPPY DAYS

These were happy days for Hergé, after a life full of constraints, whether imposed by his family, his editor, his work or the exigencies of success, as well as the difficulties brought by the war years. He finally felt himself free and, significantly for a man who was so emotionally disciplined, relaxed.

This did not mean that he created more or even better Tintin books. On the contrary, the happier and more at ease he felt at this stage, the slower his rate of production. Moreover, by leaving more work to his studio, especially his right-hand man Bob De Moor, it could be argued that there was a reduction in quality.

Certainly the string of holidays he took during the 1970s meant that he was less often in the Avenue Louise studios. Meanwhile his international audience was constantly growing and clamouring for more.

But the fact that over the best part of fifty years he had dispatched Tintin to almost every corner of the globe – as well as the Moon! – investigating a wide range of topical issues, did not leave him with an abundance of choice for new subjects. A look through the archives, at the amount of material he gathered on the continent of Australia, its marsupials and Aborigines, the modern architecture of its parliamentary capital Canberra, suggests that he toyed with the idea of sending Tintin there. In fact the original French title for *Flight 714* is *Vol 714 pour Sydney*, and Tintin and Captain Haddock, accompanied by Professor Calculus, are scheduled to disembark at Sydney for a congress but are skyjacked on the way. The final plate of the adventure has them resuming the journey and boarding Qantas Flight 714 to Sydney. The same adventure also satisfied to some extent – at least at its beginning – Hergé's attraction to an airport setting.

The idea he finally settled upon for the next Tintin adventure, however, following the mixed reception given to *Tintin and the Picaros*, was a potential winner. *Tintin and Alph-Art* was to be about the art world, with its galleries and dealers, about abstract and conceptual art as well as forgery – topics in which Hergé himself was engrossed – and to be peopled by a susceptible artist, a mysterious guru and a fashionable religious sect. He was to cast his net wide and bring together a host of characters from previous adventures. It was a project full of promise, and Hergé finally embarked on it with a gusto not seen for some time.

Tintin and Alph-Art was to be about the art world, with its galleries and dealers, a mysterious guru and a fashionable religious sect.

THE ADVENTURES OF HERGÉ, CREATOR OF TINTIN

Tintin's fiftieth anniversary celebrations in 1979 were, however, to prove a major disruption to the creative process. By the time Hergé emerged from them at the end of the year, he was physically shattered, completely exhausted. That winter Fanny took him to Igels, an Austrian resort near Innsbruck, for him to rest and recover. He took a photograph of the village band in traditional Tyrolean dress, but could manage little else. His fatigue was so extreme that the doctors were called in. Conveniently there was a clinic nearby with a specialist haematologist. Hergé was examined and given a lumbar puncture. Osteomyelofibrosis was diagnosed and regular blood transfusions were seen as the only means of countering the extreme anaemia it brought on. The holiday was cut short and he was rushed by ambulance back to Brussels for treatment.

ONLY A LITTLE TIME LEFT

At first the transfusions helped and, regaining a degree of energy, he could continue *Alph-Art*, but between transfusions he would flag again and found he could only work sporadically. The project lost momentum. By the time the longed-for reunion with Chang was due in March 1981, Hergé, once more in the public eye, was visibly a wreck, a pale shadow of his former ebullient self. He had another two years left, enough time to see Tintin trapped in an impossible predicament forty-two pages into *Alph-Art*, about to be cast as a living statue at the behest of what must be his old arch-enemy Rastapopoulos, heavily disguised as the guru Enddadine Akass, but not long enough to have the redoubtable reporter rescued. ∎

LEFT
By the time the longed-for reunion with Chang was due in March 1981, Hergé, once more in the public eye, was visibly a wreck, a pale shadow of his former ebullient self.

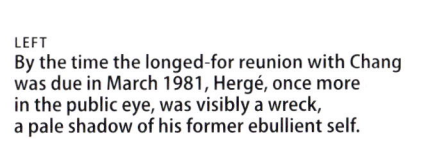

RIGHT
Detail of a cover illustration for *Le Petit Vingtième*.

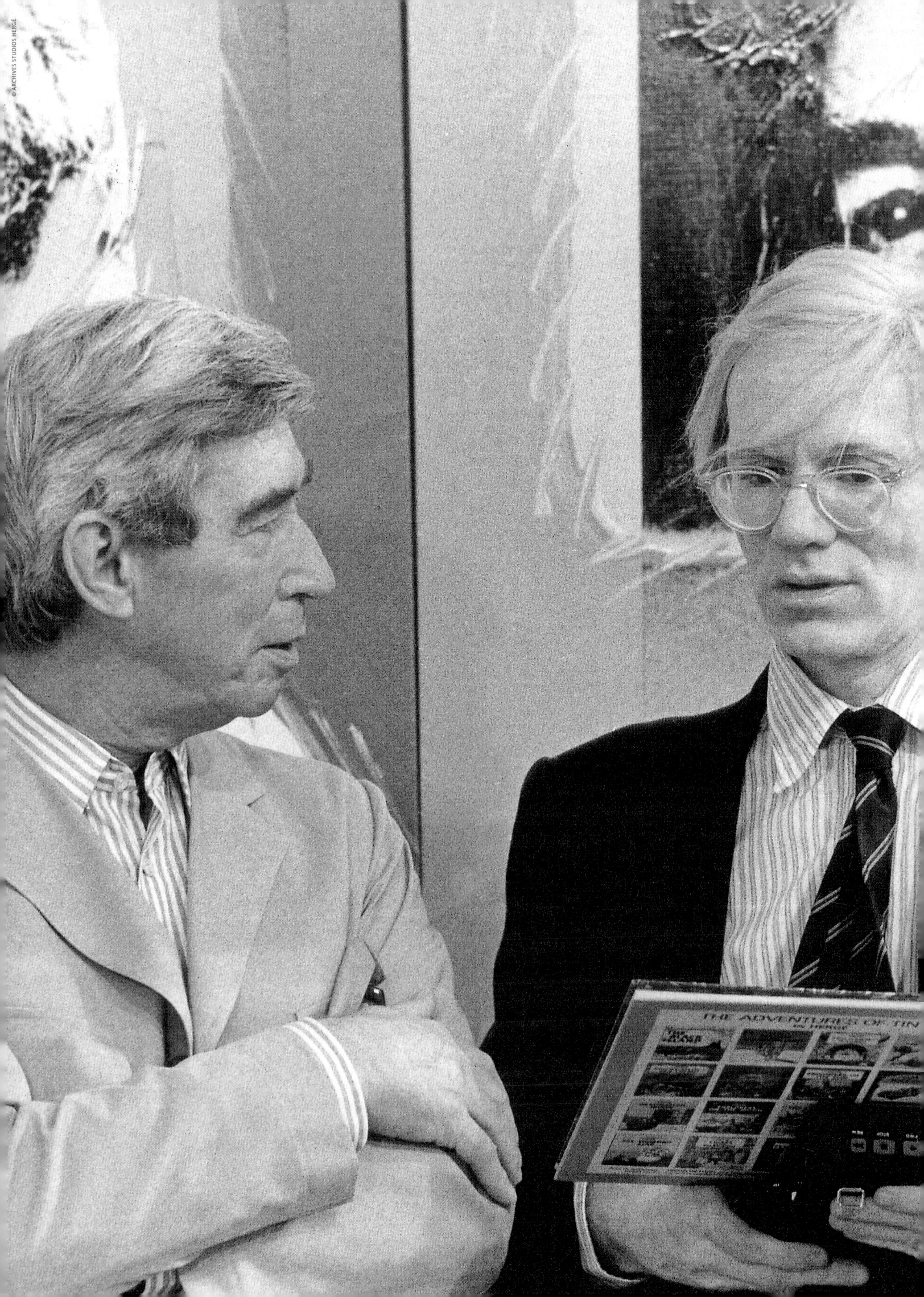
THE ADVENTURES OF TIN

CHAPTER TWO

A passion for art

Georges Remi, alias Hergé, was passionate about quite a few things, but none more than art. From an early age, with little encouragement, he had an urge to express himself in drawing. When the family visited friends, his mother would give him some crayons and paper to keep him occupied. It was not that he grew up surrounded by art and beautiful things. On the contrary, there was little of beauty to be found in his apparently solidly respectable, petit bourgeois background. There was no parental stimulation; his father ran a boys' outfitters shop and would have liked Georges to follow in his footsteps on completion of his schooling. Georges, who spent every possible moment drawing, had other ideas. Many years later, retired from providing school uniforms, Hergé's father ended up helping to administer his son's highly successful studios.

FIRST SCRIBBLES

The earliest surviving drawing by the young Georges is of a car and a man walking in front of a train, drawn in blue crayon on a postcard when he was about four. If the suggestive squiggles of his last drawing of Tintin for the unfinished *Alph-Art* represent the omega of his drawing, then this lively first sketch is the alpha. There are extraordinary similarities – each has a crude vigour. Georges covered his schoolbooks in drawings and doodles. Taking him to task for drawing during a lesson, his schoolmaster once asked him to repeat what he had just said, or face the consequences. The young Remi repeated word for word exactly what the master had said and was spared punishment.

Perhaps the most interesting exercise books, which no longer survive, were those from 1914 to 1918, years during which Brussels was under German occupation. Aged between seven and eleven, Hergé, according to his own account, drew at the bottom of pages and in the margins battle scenes and ambushes of the Boches by brave British Tommies, plucky Belgian soldiers and French *poilus*. There were also flying machines piloted by Allied aces shooting down German triplanes. Even at this early stage Georges yearned to tell stories through drawings.' There were tales of espionage, fantastic and accompanied by feverish chases, terrible traps and bursts of gunfire. Things that were really exciting,' he recalled later.*

These were adventures without text, as, according to Hergé, he would imagine the dialogue. 'I believe it involved a young man, a spy who ran rings around the Germans.' It sounds rather like the contemporary thrillers of John Buchan that Hergé, indirectly through the work of Alfred Hitchcock, was to discover later.

ABOVE
The earliest surviving drawing by the young Georges.

LEFT
Hergé and Andy Warhol in the Brussels studios, 1976.

* *Le Soir*, 19 December 1940.

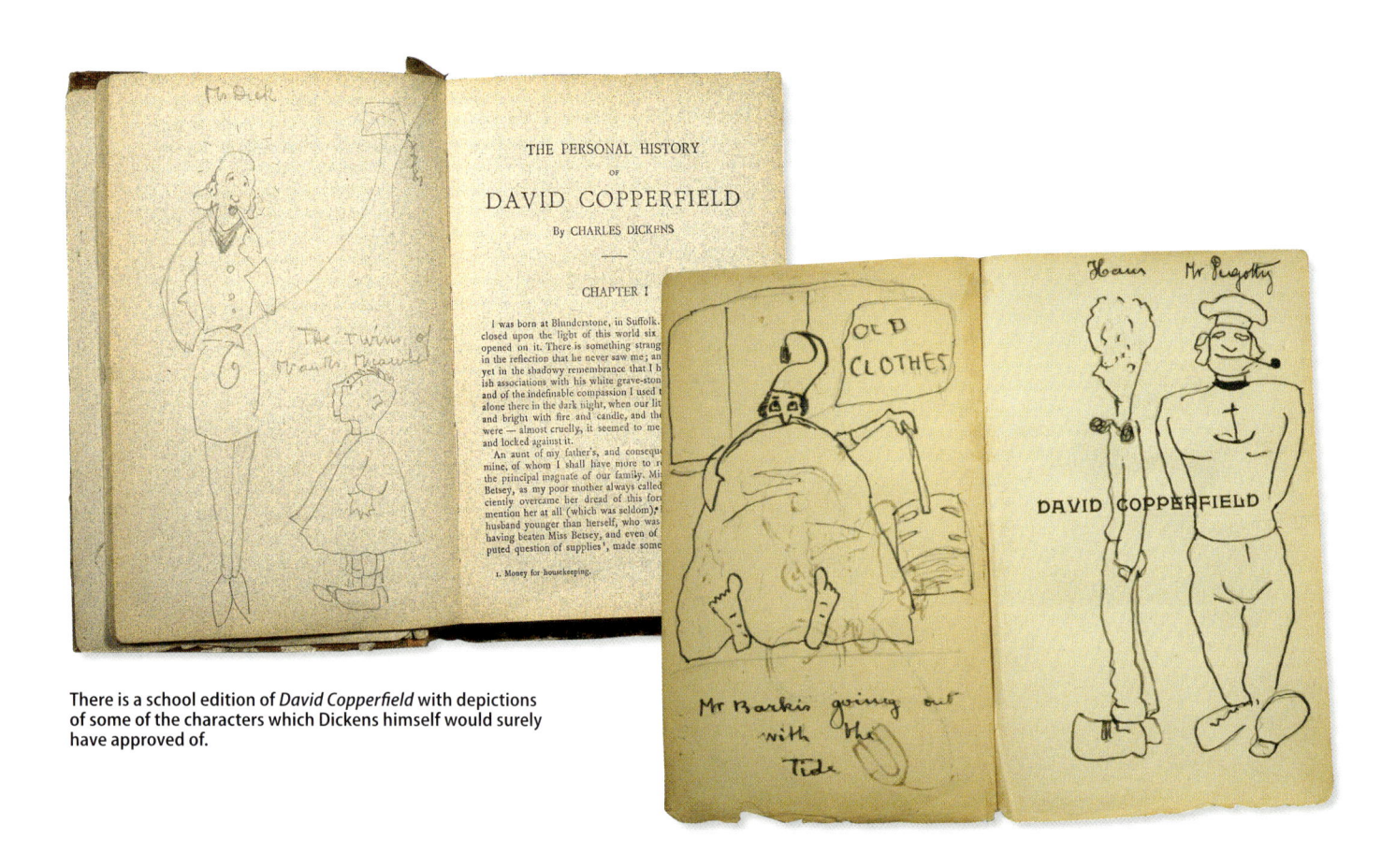

There is a school edition of *David Copperfield* with depictions of some of the characters which Dickens himself would surely have approved of.

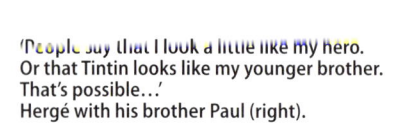

'People say that I look a little like my hero. Or that Tintin looks like my younger brother. That's possible…'
Hergé with his brother Paul (right).

Other schoolbooks that do survive are often heavily annotated or illustrated by Georges with drawings that are sometimes relevant and at other times totally irrelevant. There is a school edition of *David Copperfield* with depictions of some of the characters that Dickens himself would surely have approved of.

FIRST FEELINGS

Then there was Marie-Louise Van Cutsem's poetry book. Marie-Louise, or Milou for short, was Georges's first girlfriend, and in 1918 he provided some charming drawings for an album of poetry she kept. Other drawings dedicated to her followed over the next few years, including one of a British soldier in uniform. The long-standing friendship developed into something more, despite Milou being almost two years older and, at least physically, markedly more mature.

Georges was bitterly disappointed some time later – in 1924 – when Marie-Louise's father, who worked for the celebrated Belgian art nouveau architect Victor Horta, forbade his daughter from continuing the friendship because he believed the young Remi to be beneath her station. Furthermore, he considered him to be 'a young man with no future'.

There were consequences, for when Georges, by now known as Hergé – derived from the French pronunciation of his initials reversed to R.G. – came to invent Tintin in January 1929 he chose to call the reporter's faithful companion Milou, after the girl he had been so fond of. This allusion is, of course, lost in the English translation of *The Adventures of Tintin*, where Milou becomes Snowy because of the unusual – for a fox terrier – whiteness of his coat.

Born at 7.30 a.m. on 22 May 1907, in the Etterbeek district of Brussels, Georges Prosper Remi was the first child of Alexis and Élisabeth Remi. Five years later they were to have a second son, Paul. He, like Georges, was also to break away from the somewhat restrictive and claustrophobic home environment. Rather than sell uniforms, Paul was destined to wear them for much of his life, as a cavalry officer. Where his elder brother was passionate about drawing and art, he was keen on horses, and the army offered a suitable career for such an enthusiast.

Drawing of a British soldier in uniform, dedicated to Marie-Louise.

FAMILY RESEMBLANCES

Apart from later helping his brother to draw horses at the gallop and canter accurately, Paul played a further role in the creation of Tintin, for he had, unlike Georges, a round face and cultivated a distinctive hairstyle – a quiff. The resemblance between Paul and the hero reporter – at least after the first pages of *Tintin in the Land of the Soviets* – is so marked that his fellow officers came to call him 'Major Tintin'. This rather irritating constant reminder of his brother's success led him during the 1950s to have a radical change of haircut, with most of it shaved off in the manner of the well-known pre-war screen actor Erich von Stroheim. Hergé was not prepared to let him get away with it, creating in *The Calculus Affair* (1956) the monocled villain Colonel Sponsz – a uniformed figure of identical appearance to his recoiffured brother.

In an article that appeared in *Le Soir* in December 1940, Hergé noted: 'People say that I look a little like my hero. Or that Tintin looks like my younger brother. That's possible... All I can say is that during my childhood I had as a playmate a brother who was five years younger than me. I observed him a lot. He amused and fascinated me. (Today he is a prisoner of war in a Stalag.*) And that, no doubt, is the explanation of why Tintin borrowed his character, his gestures and attitudes.'

---

* Captured during the invasion of Belgium in May 1940, Paul Remi spent the war years as a prisoner in a camp for officers in Nazi Germany.

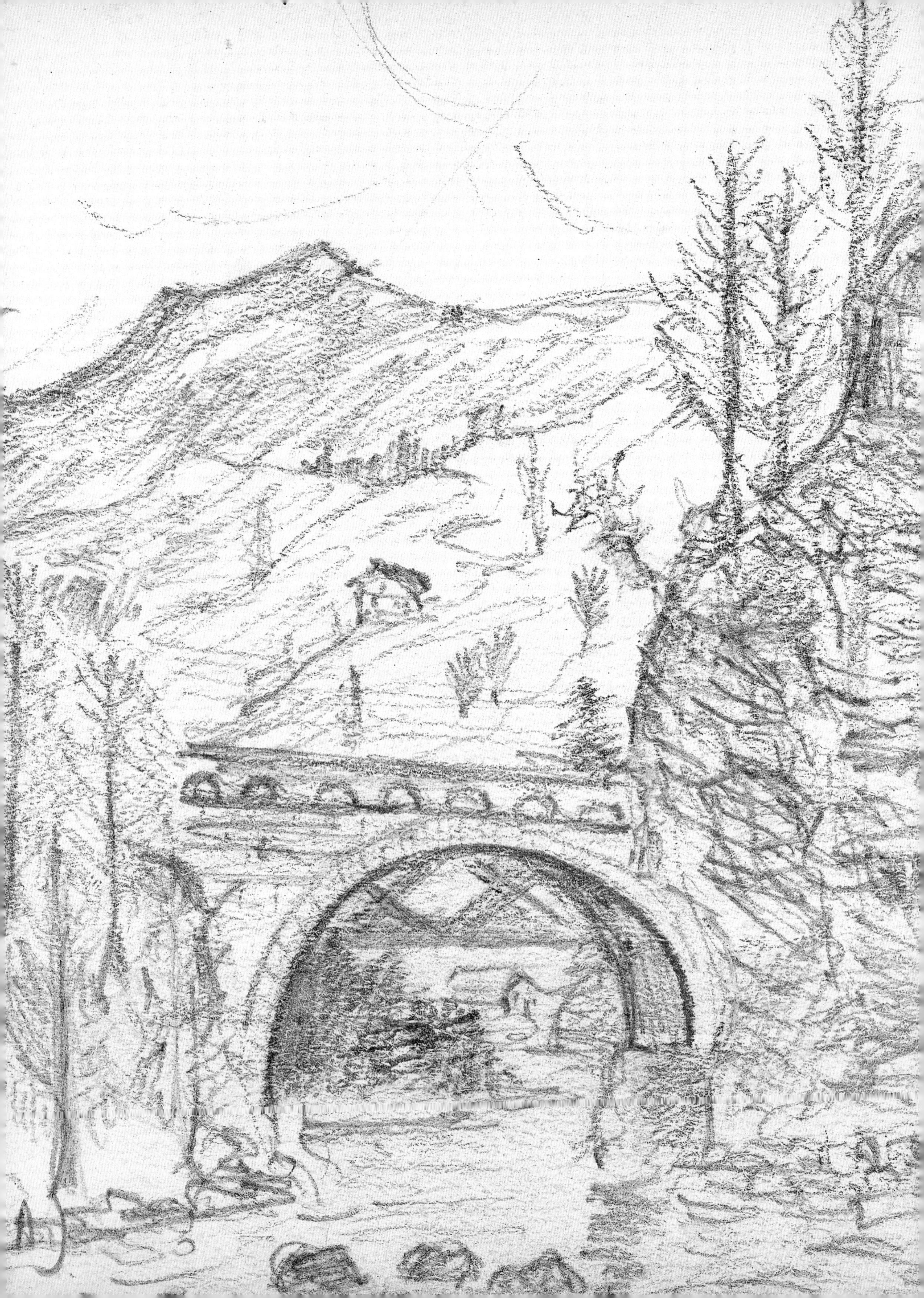

CHAPTER TWO **A PASSION FOR ART**

LEFT
On scouting expeditions, Hergé could draw sensitive landscapes.

ABOVE
Hergé's father Alexis and his uncle Léon, who were identical twins, provided inspiration for the Thom(p)sons.

BELOW
Elegantly dressed young man at the races.

When it came to Tintin, Hergé did not let his family and friends off lightly. If Paul was Tintin, and Milou was Snowy, then his father Alexis and his uncle Léon, who were identical twins, provided the inspiration for the Thom(p)sons, who are so remarkably similar (only the shape of their moustaches differing slightly), though with that crucial difference in the spelling of their surnames – one 'with a p, as in psychology' – they cannot, of course, be twins.

The Remi twin brothers were also inseparable. For some time they sported similar moustaches and dressed in the same manner. They would meet invariably for a Sunday walk, when they would venture forth in their best suits and bowler hats, carrying walking canes or, if inclement weather threatened, black umbrellas. Georges needed to look no farther for inspiration.

Hergé's aversion to opera, and the inspiration for Bianca Castafiore, his leading lady – 'the Milanese Nightingale' – is understood, moreover, to have derived from a maternal aunt, Ninie, who endeavoured not altogether successfully to entertain the Remi family with her squally singing. Later he recalled additionally being taken regularly by his parents to visit friends whose daughter's singing would 'terrorise' him.

The young Hergé chose all sorts of subjects for his drawing – soldiers in uniform, Native Americans by their tepees, a particularly grisly-looking Bolshevik years before Tintin was to encounter his like in his debut adventure, a black jazz band, elegantly dressed young men at the races or standing poised by their touring cars in the manner of a Dornford Yates novel, figures in historical dress, the odd musketeer, and, on his scouting expeditions, some sensitive landscapes.

His parents responded to his delight in drawing by enrolling him for art classes. But one session sufficed; he was asked to copy a Corinthian capital, a task he found too tedious to continue. His imagination had to be fired, and the prospect of tame still lifes was not for him, either then or later. In his maturity, it was abstract and even conceptual art which he found particularly compelling.

ESCAPE TO THE OPEN AIR!

It was Hergé's love of scouting, providing him with such welcome relief from the boredom at home,* which was to provide him with the bulk of his subject matter for drawing during his teenage years. It was also to see him published for the first time, and on a regular basis, for his drawings in a wide variety of shapes and forms were welcome embellishments to *Le Boy-Scout Belge*, to which he became a regular contributor from 1923 onwards. It was, moreover, a template for his work on the Catholic newspaper *Le Vingtième Siècle* after he left school, where, although initially employed in the subscriptions department, his talent for drawing allowed him to escape its drudgery and provide artwork for various sections of the paper. In effect, he was paid to furnish exactly the sort of drawings he had executed for his pleasure during his schooldays.

Meanwhile, for *Le Boy-Scout Belge* he moved farther towards the strip cartoon with his creation of a resourceful scout called Totor, whose adventures appeared in its pages between 1926 and 1929. When in the autumn of 1928 the forceful director of *Le Vingtième Siècle*, Father Norbert Wallez, suddenly put him in charge of a children's supplement, to be called *Le Petit*

ABOVE
Scouting provided Georges with a welcome relief from the boredom at home.

* In an interview in the French newspaper *Le Monde* in February 1973, Hergé recalled: 'My childhood seemed to me very grey. Of course I have memories, but these do not begin to brighten, to become coloured until the moment when I discovered scouting.'

CHAPTER TWO **A PASSION FOR ART**

Vingtième, Hergé began by illustrating other contributors' stories, but soon realised he needed something more substantial to fill the pages. By January 1929 he thought of relating the adventures of a young reporter – which no doubt Hergé would have liked to be himself – whom, recalling the catchy alliteration of his scout hero Totor, he would call Tintin.

There is another possible explanation for the alliterative choice. Friends of his from school and scouting, the Delville brothers, had been in England during the war years and had returned with copies of a children's illustrated comic, *The Rainbow*, in which there was a strip cartoon with a heroic tiger called Tiger Tim. Georges borrowed the comic and clearly the repetition of the letter 't' appealed to him and made an impression. The French word 'Tintin!', meaning 'ring' or 'tinkle', does not seem to have had any particular relevance, though it would later provide an amusing pun when, as on page 7 of *King Ottokar's Sceptre*, visitors rang the doorbell marked 'Tintin' for the reporter's flat.

Prior to Tintin, Hergé's drawings had accompanied and illustrated texts, but with the creation of the reporter he was to take the development of the strip cartoon farther with the introduction of speech bubbles, something he had discovered in the revelatory comic strips he found in American newspapers, as well as the pioneering work – dating from 1925 – of the Frenchman Alain Saint-Ogan in his *Adventures of Zig and Puce*, in which a pair of ungainly young heroes and their penguin friend Alfred travel the world together. Hergé came across the American newspapers in the offices of *Le Vingtième Siècle*, where they had been sent by the newspaper's correspondent in Mexico, Léon Degrelle, later to become notorious as the Belgian fascist or 'Rexist' leader.

With Tintin, therefore, Hergé was breaking new ground – certainly in Europe – by blending together images and narrative into fast-paced adventures. There was an obvious parallel with the rapid evolution at the time of the cinema – notably the move from the silent to the spoken film, for 1929 was the year of the 'talkies' – but the strip cartoon as developed by Hergé also drew heavily on the latest trends in contemporary art. In this respect, the first Tintin adventure, *Tintin in the Land of the Soviets*, which began to unfold in the pages of *Le Petit Vingtième* on 10 January 1929, was itself abreast of modern art.

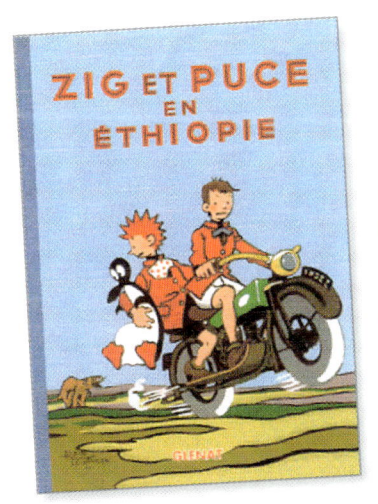

ABOVE
A pair of ungainly young heroes and their penguin friend Alfred travel the world together.

BELOW
For *Le Boy-Scout Belge* he moved farther towards the strip cartoon with his creation of a resourceful scout called Totor.

The first Tintin adventure, *Tintin in the Land of the Soviets*, began to unfold in the pages of *Le Petit Vingtième* on 10 January 1929.

THE ADVENTURES OF HERGÉ, CREATOR OF TINTIN

ABOVE
In an extraordinary experimental and daring move Hergé blacks out a whole frame in the Soviet adventure.

RIGHT
Movement could be captured by repeating lines or images and through distortion.

BELOW
Tintin slamming his foot on the accelerator of the Mercedes-Benz tourer and his hair being swept up into the distinctive style.

A NEW FORM OF LITERATURE AND ART

The Soviet adventure was still largely experimental and at times imperfect, which is why years later Hergé was reluctant to have it republished, and then only in a facsimile edition rather than the updated format of the other books. Apart from Moscow, Hergé was not quite sure where Tintin was going in this first adventure, allowing the narrative and drawings to find their own way from one week to the next in a hectic, helter-skelter manner. The rigorous documentary research and routine that were to become characteristic of the creation of later Tintin adventures had yet to become a habit. Instead, there was an abundance of spontaneity – the way, for example, that Tintin's quiff suddenly appears. Hergé liked the effect, induced by Tintin slamming his foot on the accelerator of the Mercedes-Benz tourer and his hair being swept up into the distinctive style, and kept it from then on. Sometimes the drawings have all the immediacy of the first thought and sketch, an electricity of line. It is a long and exhausting journey, but by the time the reporter returns to Brussels at its end, Hergé has learned how to create a Tintin adventure while readers have discovered an exciting new form of literature and art. A model now existed and a pattern was being worked out which could be continued in the next adventure, *Tintin in the Congo*, and especially the subsequent *Tintin in America*, which Hergé meant as the capitalist pendant to the opening exposé of communism.

For a twenty-one-year-old, as Hergé still was in early 1929, the first Tintin adventure shows a remarkable awareness of all that was new in art. Untrained as either an artist or an art historian, Hergé could yet demonstrate his credentials in both disciplines.

The year 1912 proved to be a key date in the history of art, for suddenly half a dozen leading European artists turned from figurative to abstract art. In Paris, Pablo Picasso and Georges Braque, having developed Cubism out of the thrilling example of Cézanne's late work, had reached the limits of depicting objects. Also in Paris, Robert Delaunay's depiction of light and the colours of the spectrum made only the barest references to such modern symbols as the Eiffel Tower. In Germany the Moscow-born Vasily Kandinsky, in Prague Frantisek Kupka and in Russia Kasimir Malevich all broke the abstract barrier in the succeeding months. That, however, did not mean that their work was particularly well known beyond their own circles until years later. For Hergé, working outside the artistic mainstream in Brussels, to have been familiar even in 1929 with the early abstract work of Malevich is remarkable. Yet in an extraordinary experimental and daring move he blacks out a whole frame in the Soviet adventure – a room plunged into darkness – to form a black square in the manner of Malevich's celebrated abstraction of that name. In terms of the new, developing art of the strip cartoon it is both a conceit and a tour de force, showing nothing in the place of movement and action, halting the lateral flow of the visual narrative, arresting its progress. But while breaking all the apparent rules of this art form, it works wonderfully in creating suspense and a profound sense of anxiety.

Black Square.
Kasimir Malevich, 1913, oil on canvas.
Russian State Museum, St Petersburg.

ART IN MOTION

Similarly, the first Tintin adventure shows an awareness of the Italian Futurists with their love of speed and machines and their depiction of motion and velocity. Artists such as Umberto Boccioni and Giacomo Balla – with, for example, his painting of a dachshund being walked in the street, *Leash in Motion*, 1912 – provided examples of how movement could be captured by repeating lines or images and through distortion, offering formulae that were ideally suited for adaptation to the strip cartoon. When Tintin bends strenuously up and down to propel the hand-powered railcar, Hergé repeats the outline of his back to capture the movement, following the Futurist example. There are further instances throughout *The Adventures of Tintin*, whether it is Snowy in a frantic spin with a parrot or Nestor busy with his feather duster (*Tintin and the Picaros*, page 11), to take just two examples.

Hergé was already demonstrating his extraordinary openness to new ideas and trends and his ability to assimilate them when they could prove useful. He admitted that he was able to absorb ideas like a sponge, a quality he retained to the end. The result was that whether at the beginning or the close of his career, he was always aware of the latest developments and consequently remarkably 'with it'.

In his last unfinished work, *Tintin and Alph-Art*, the contemporary art scene actually becomes the subject. Captain Haddock, normally so conservative, astoundingly becomes a conceptual art enthusiast, purchasing a large letter 'H' sculpture for Marlinspike, and the 'compressions' and 'expansions' of the sculptor César* feature, with Tintin apparently doomed to become an 'expansion' of his by having liquid polyester poured over him.

His early knowledge of abstract art was to spur a lifelong fascination. While much later, in the years leading up to *Tintin and Alph-Art*, he could keep up with the latest trends through his almost daily contact with Marcel Stal at the Carrefour Gallery, as a young man there were no such possibilities. There was not yet any contemporary art in public collections, and there were very few modern galleries, with most collectors buying directly from artists. So what Hergé would have known about Malevich, Balla and modern art in general would have been gleaned from the newspapers, journals and magazines that he was forever combing for raw material. Nevertheless, he was unusually well informed.

Later, friendships were to mould his artistic taste. When in October 1940 he joined Belgium's leading French-language daily *Le Soir*, he got to know Jacques Van Melkebeke, a Brussels artist working on the children's section of the newspaper. Van Melkebeke, who in 1945 painted an oil portrait** of Hergé in profile, pencil in hand poised above a sketch of Tintin and Snowy, was a talented, though far from avant-garde, artist. Some of his painting could be distinctly erotic. He had firm views on what was good and bad in art which certainly influenced Hergé. He also read widely, and Hergé would seem to have picked up indirectly through him ideas from authors he may not have read himself for use in *The Adventures of Tintin*.

ABOVE
Captain Haddock astoundingly becomes a conceptual art enthusiast, purchasing a large letter 'H' sculpture for Marlinspike.

BELOW
Modigliani, Léger, Renoir, Picasso, Gauguin and Monet – discovered by Tintin in the villa of the mysterious Enddadine Akass on Capri.

---

*   The French sculptor César Baldaccini, born in 1921 and better known as César.
** For many years it hung in the front room of his home.

CHAPTER TWO **A PASSION FOR ART**

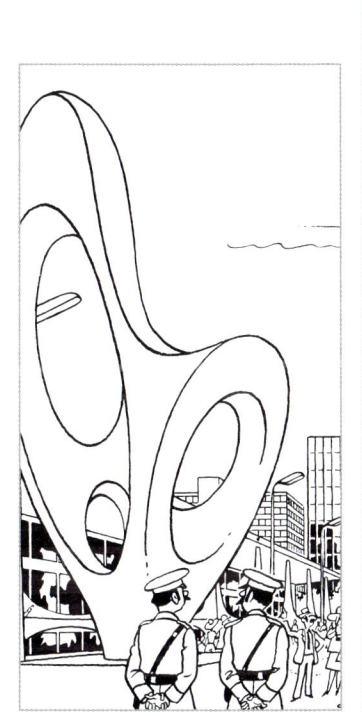

ART THROUGHOUT

ABOVE
In *Tintin and the Picaros* the streets of Tapiocapolis offer a setting for the sculpture of Marcel Arnould and the government guest house a wall to hang an abstract painting by Serge Poliakoff (see the painting belonging to Hergé illustrated on page 37).

Art is, moreover, occasionally referred to directly in the Tintin books. The heavy shadows of the colonnaded streets of Las Dopicos depicted in *The Broken Ear* are strongly reminiscent of paintings by the Italian surrealist artist Giorgio de Chirico, notably his *Place d'Italie* of 1912 or *Melancholy* of 1913, while a version of the Impressionist Alfred Sisley's *Le Canal du Loing* from the Louvre collection can be clearly identified hanging at Marlinspike Hall in *The Red Sea Sharks* (page 10) as Nestor the butler brings the Thom(p)sons their bowler hats and canes. On page 36 of the same adventure, there is no mistaking the contemporaneous Picasso which Rastapopoulos, alias the Marquis di Gorgonzola, has hanging on his cabin wall. Later, in *Flight 714*, the unsmiling billionaire Laszlo Carreidas seeks to outbid Aristotle Onassis at a Parke-Bennet auction in New York to acquire three Picassos, two Braques and a Renoir, despite not having 'an inch of space to hang them'. In *Tintin and the Picaros* the streets of Tapiocapolis offer a setting for the sculpture of Marcel Arnould (page 11) and the government guest house a wall to hang an abstract painting by Serge Poliakoff (page 14), an artist much admired by Hergé and included in his personal art collection. In the final, unfinished *Tintin and Alph-Art*, there is a cornucopia of modern art, from conceptualism to the expansions of César via the long list of forgeries of modern masters – Modigliani, Léger, Renoir, Picasso, Gauguin and Monet – discovered by Tintin in the villa of the mysterious Enddadine Akass on Capri. In Hergé's draft drawing illustrating this episode, the Modigliani and its signature can be clearly made out – one of his alluringly languid elongated females – the Picasso is only a couple of squiggles and he has not yet worked out the others. He also has Akass showing Tintin examples of the sculptor César's compressions and expansions as he explains the fearful fate he plans for the reporter.

As a collector, Hergé, according to his own account, loved to surround himself with pictures and art. 'I cannot live without paintings around me,' he admitted towards the end of his life. Initially his taste was predictably conventional, even if he was aware of the latest developments in modern art. The homes he shared with his first wife Germaine were decorated with heavy Flemish furniture and innocuous landscapes, as well as his portrait by Van Melkebeke. Subsequently he was drawn to the work of the Flemish Expressionists, such as Constant Permeke (1886–1952; wounded at the front in 1914, he spent some time in England before returning to settle near Ostend) and Jakob Smits, but it was the friendship and almost daily contact with the gallery owner Marcel Stal which brought the real breakthrough and his unashamed espousal of abstract art. Furthermore, establishing home with Fanny Vlamynck, who in due course would become his second wife, coincided happily with this new enthusiasm. The new homes they occupied were furnished in a very much more modern manner, as if he was determined to clear away the fustiness of the past. Fanny herself, moreover, shared his excitement over and attraction to the latest art and design.

Already, in March 1957, in reply to questions posed by a woman's magazine – *Femmes d'Aujourd'hui* (Women of Today) – he spoke of abstract art and 'feeling the need of a shock, of a breath of fresh air'. He told how he had introduced the latest designer furniture into the studios, such as the Harry Bertoia bench that can still be seen and used just inside the entrance to the Studios Hergé, and which features on page 17 of *Tintin and the Picaros*, where Captain Haddock falls back and knocks it over.

CUTTING-EDGE ART

Hergé had long been a fervent admirer of the Spanish painter Miró – probably his favourite artist – and possessed an example of his work, but now, encouraged by Stal, he ranged more widely. The Italian-Argentinian Lucio Fontana (1899–1968), with his delicately slashed canvases, became a particular favourite, as well as Serge Poliakoff. Born in Moscow in 1906 – the year before Hergé – Poliakoff began as a guitarist, settled in Paris in 1923 and took up painting seven years later. His work is remarkable for its interlocked shapes and colour harmonies. Some critics compared his use of colour to the early Venetian masters, and Hergé was the proud owner of three of his paintings.

Hergé could sit for hours contemplating the Fontanas in his collection,* works that, according to Fanny, he found 'very Zen', mirroring his deep interest in Zen Buddhism and philosophy. Fontana, the son of a sculptor, transcended the confines of two-dimensional painting with first his *Buchi* (holes) series of 1949 and then his *taglio* (slash) paintings from 1958. Influenced by the Italian Futurist movement's interest in states of being, he had in his *White Manifesto* of 1946 set out the goals for a 'spatialist art' that would engage material to achieve an expression of a new dimension – space. The first punctured canvas followed three years later, exploring the relationship between space and matter, as well as creating a painting that was not merely a surface but an object. This was art, he claimed, that had relevance for the age of technology and space travel – of obvious appeal to the modernistic Hergé. 'I am seeking to represent the void,' Fontana declared.

He would have liked to buy a painting by Mark Rothko but in the end decided it was too expensive. He acquired a sculpture by Alexander Calder, the originator during the 1930s of

---

* Hergé came to possess four canvases by Fontana: one large, one medium sized and two small.

CHAPTER TWO **A PASSION FOR ART**

'stabiles' and 'mobiles', and discovered the coloured fluorescent light creations of the American minimalist Dan Flavin, again obtaining an example. Flavin (1933–96) made ethereal works out of fluorescent lighting tubes that fill their space with colour or pure white light. Among foreign holiday snaps he took during the 1970s is one of Fanny beside a work by Calder. He was clearly completely smitten by modern art, though less unexpectedly than Captain Haddock when he succumbs to and purchases Ramo Nash's letter H sculpture in *Tintin and Alph-Art*.

The photographer André Soupart took a sensitive sequence of pictures of Hergé posing with pieces from his collection, demonstrating his enthusiasm and affection for the art he surrounded himself with.

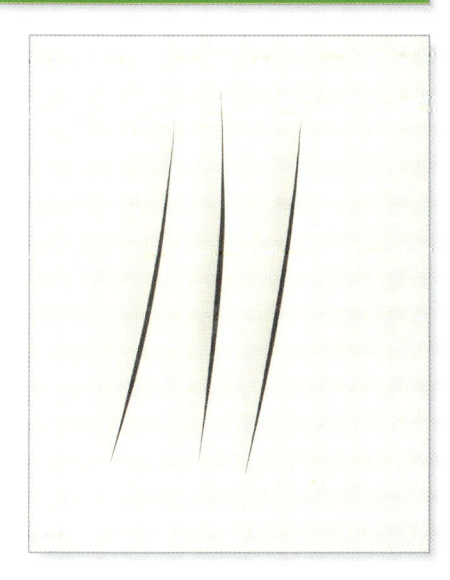

BELOW LEFT
Paintings from Hergé's collection: Serge Poliakoff, Tonning Rasmüssen and Lucio Fontana.

BELOW RIGHT
Photograph of Hergé talking passionately of art, taken by André Soupart.

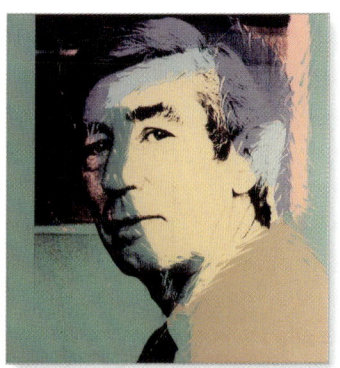

AND POP ART

Hergé had known Marcel Stal since the early 1930s when he was a friend of his brother Paul at the School of Artillery and, like him, embarking on a career as a soldier. It was Stal in those pre-war days who introduced him to the memorable expletive '*Tonnerre de Brest!*', which Hergé remembered for Captain Haddock when he brought him into the series in 1940, and which is well translated in the English editions as '*Thundering typhoons!*' Stal was already then an art enthusiast, though not especially interested in strip cartoons. Of *The Adventures of Tintin*, it was only *The Castafiore Emerald* which he really cared for, sharing the view of many who consider it to be a tour de force. When in 1960 he retired from the army as a colonel, Hergé helped him set up the art gallery he had long wanted, conveniently a few doors along from the Studios Hergé in the Avenue Louise. Hergé paid the first three months' rent for the Carrefour Gallery and became a regular visitor there, arriving almost daily during the week at 12.05 p.m. precisely for his '*petit french*' or dry martini cocktail of gin and a hint of vermouth (Noilly Prat to be precise), shaken not stirred, and a chance to chat with artists, critics and collectors. As always with Hergé it was an opportunity to learn, and he soaked up all he could about trends and developments.

The 1960s marked the beginnings of pop art, a movement of obvious mutual appeal to Hergé, with his love of 'the clear line', and leading exponents such as Andy Warhol and Roy Lichtenstein. Warhol, whose 'Factory' in New York Hergé visited in 1972 and who completed a series of screen portraits of the creator of Tintin, could declare: 'Hergé influenced my work as much as Disney . . . He had great political and satirical dimensions.' For his part Hergé could draw on material by Warhol for Tintin. There are, for example, marked similarities between Hergé's drawings of a car accident for an aborted Tintin project in the early 1960s and Warhol's 'Saturday Disaster' sequence (1964). The two artists renewed their acquaintance in Brussels in 1976 when the Warhol portraits of Hergé went on display.

As for Lichtenstein, Hergé found a similarity in their working methods, particularly at the initial stages, and in what he called the 'readability' of their work. He described the American as 'certainly one of the greatest artists of our epoch'.

For his part, Lichtenstein acknowledged his appreciation by depicting Tintin in his flat in Labrador Road. He pictures the reporter sitting in his favourite red armchair reading the newspaper, Snowy at his feet, as a dagger whizzes by and a door slams, disturbing the peace dangerously. The scene is a very free interpretation of an episode on page 8 of *The Broken Ear*. The naval cap of Captain Haddock, whom Tintin had not yet met this far into *The Adventures*, rests on a small table and Henri Matisse's seminal painting *La Danse* hangs on the wall, signifying a double tribute by the American pop artist.

ABOVE
The two artists renewed their acquaintance in Brussels in 1976 when the Warhol portraits of Hergé went on display.

Although Hergé did not manage to meet Lichtenstein, he did acquire his screenprint series of Rouen cathedral inspired by Claude Monet, and the delicately beautiful pictures happily confront the sensitive trio of Warhol portraits on the facing wall of his former office in the Avenue Louise, today the meeting room of the Studios Hergé.

Art and Hergé's taste for it had progressed by leaps and bounds from the charming but tame 1945 Van Melkebeke portrait. Yet it was Van Melkebeke who had really set the process in motion with the help of Hergé's art-collecting tailor Van Geluwe, an aficionado of modern Belgian art, and, of course, Marcel Stal. Important roles were also played by Guy Debruyne, who specialised in American artists, minimalists and conceptual art at his gallery 'D', and a young art critic, Pierre Sterckx, whom Hergé met and befriended at Carrefour in 1965.

Hergé was delighted to meet Sterckx, an academic immersed in his pet subjects of art, philosophy and jazz, and offered him a fee – which he refused – to come weekly to his home and talk about them. As in previous instances, such as his contact with the scientist Bernard Heuvelmans, it was an example of Hergé seeking out an expert from whom he could learn, in this case about the aesthetics of art. Having never trained as an artist or art historian, he felt he had much ground to make up. Apart from their weekly discussions, the two men would go to exhibitions and museums to seek out examples of art they could consider.

ARTISTIC TASTE

Among the Old Masters, Hergé would single out as his preferred painters Jan Vermeer (1632–75) of Delft and Pieter Bruegel (c.1520–69), whose works he admired for their clarity. He found the work of Hieronymus Bosch (c.1460–1516) to be admirably clear too, even if the symbolism was complex. As the foremost champion of '*la ligne claire*' (clear line) among strip cartoonists, he could not help but admire the superb draughtsmanship and line of Jean Auguste Dominique Ingres (1780–1867) among nineteenth-century masters.

During the early 1960s Hergé's enthusiasm for abstract art fuelled a desire, moreover, for him to try painting canvases himself. Again he sought instruction and advice; this time from the abstract artist Louis Van Lint. He too would visit Hergé's home to give lessons. Initially under Van Lint's supervision and then on his own, Hergé completed thirty-seven abstract paintings strongly influenced by Miró and Poliakoff. Although not without merit, the venture was hardly an unqualified success. For an opinion, Hergé took examples of his work as an abstract painter to Léo Van Puyvelde, chief curator of the Beaux-Arts museums in Belgium, whose advice was that he should continue with what he was famous for – *The Adventures of Tintin*.

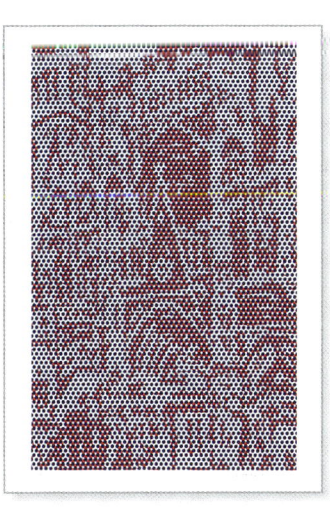

Although Hergé did not manage to meet Lichtenstein, he did acquire his screenprint series of Rouen cathedral inspired by Claude Monet.

Hergé was discouraged and, according to Fanny, deciding that he did not want to be merely a weekend painter – it was a question of all or nothing – gave up his ambitions and relegated his canvases to the attic. One work, however, prospered more – Marcel Stal took it in exchange for a canvas by Fontana. Hergé had painted in oils before, though not abstract works. There is a pastel-hued portrait of his first wife Germaine, rather in the manner, if less accomplished, of Van Melkebeke's portrait of Hergé. It is naive and conservative, feminine and charming, reminiscent too of the delightful paintings by the French artist Marie de Laurencin. There are also sensitive watercolours by Hergé of his beloved Siamese cats, and again of Germaine.

If he was overly modest about his efforts at painting, there is no doubt about his ability with pencil and pen and his strong sense of graphic design. Before it became certain that Tintin would take over his career, during the 1930s he set up the Atelier Hergé, which carried through with panache a variety of commissions for advertising, book design and typography. Again he was thoroughly aware of current trends that were to be flagposted at the Bauhaus by artists such as Laszlo Moholy-Nagy and Josef Albers. Quite apart from the breakthrough he brought to the strip cartoon with Tintin, the typography used in the adventures – notably the book covers and title pages – was carefully thought out, distinctive and innovative. During the 1930s he experimented with a variety of techniques for his book illustrations and advertising work, including some highly effective drawings using broad areas of black ink starkly contrasting with white, in the manner of old woodcuts or more modern linocuts. A striking example is to be found in the illustrations he provided for *The Story of Albert I, King of the Belgians*, published by Casterman in 1934.

TOP AND ABOVE
Hergé experimented with a variety of techniques for his book illustrations and advertising work, including some highly effective drawings using broad areas of black ink starkly contrasting with white, in the manner of old woodcuts or more modern linocuts.

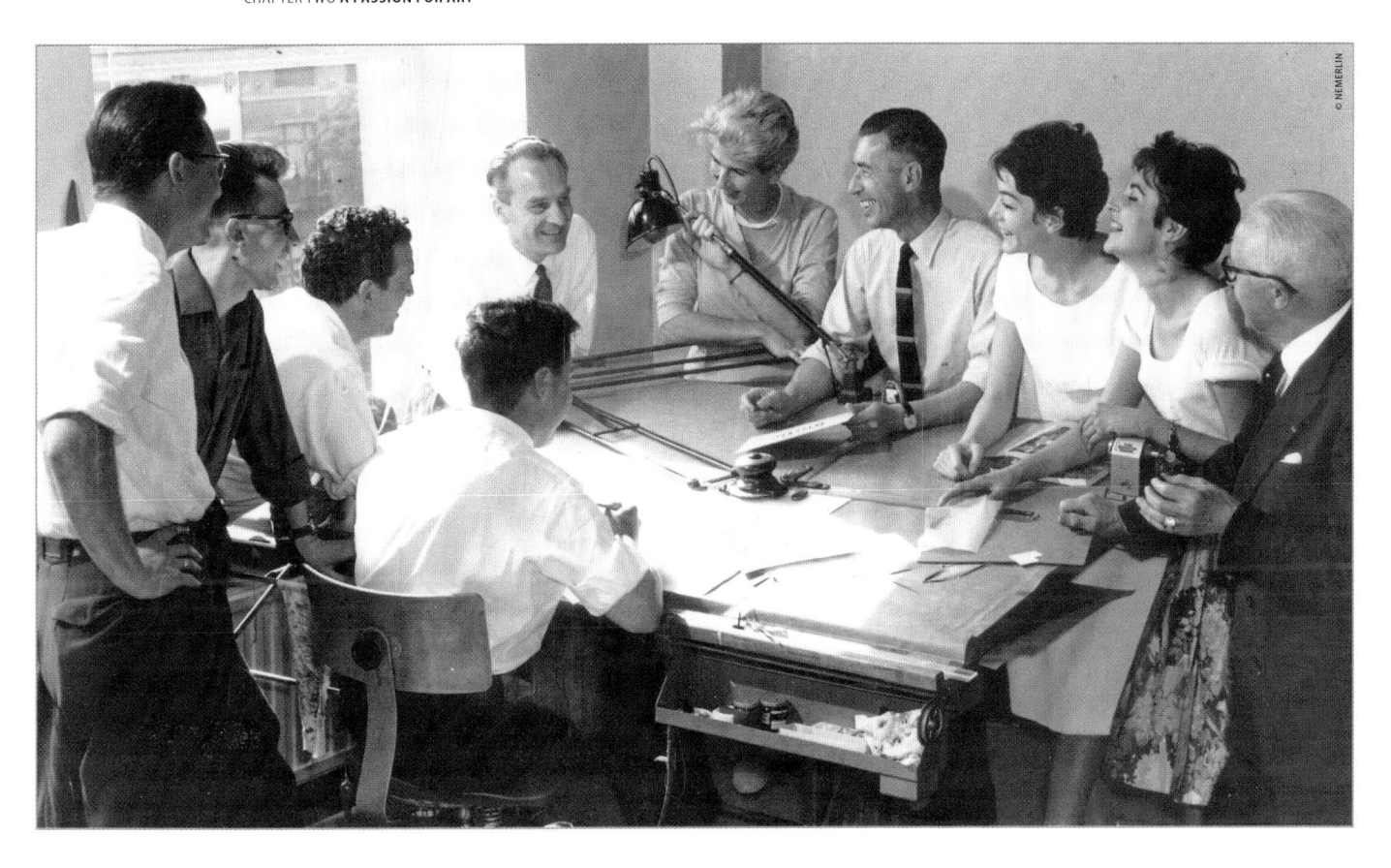

In 1950 Hergé set up the Studios Hergé where he gathered a competent team to help him sort out the runaway success of Tintin.

The runaway success of Tintin, however, left him with little time for other work. Producing Tintin became a full-time job in itself and eventually more than Hergé could cope with on his own. So in 1950 he set up, initially at number 194 and a little later at 162 Avenue Louise, a modern office block, the Studios Hergé, where he would gather together a team of fellow strip cartoonists, colourists and a secretary/personal assistant to handle correspondence and administration. Hergé remained very much in charge, but he was able to delegate time-consuming tasks such as colouring or drawing background scenes, motor vehicles, aeroplanes and other detail, as well as subsidiary characters, to members of the team, each a specialist in a particular area. He would continue his principal role as author/artist while supervising their work. The studios could, moreover, handle advertising commissions such as those promoting the drinking of milk (part of a government campaign), Nutella spread, Lesieur sunflower oil, Salik anoraks or the Thom(p)sons' association with the Citroën 2CV. Hergé made a point of carefully vetting all advertising requests for their suitability.

AN ARTISTIC ALL-ROUNDER

When it came to art Hergé was an all-rounder, even if he could not achieve the high goals he may later have set himself as an abstract artist. Like everything he did, even this experiment helped his understanding and quest for knowledge. He dedicated his life to art – his passion – which he appreciated in many forms and desired around him, whether the costly antique Chinese vases he purchased in London, the work of Warhol and Lichtenstein which he acquired, or the radiant golden Buddha he bought from a Tibetan monk. His own desire to draw was an instinctive means of expression from a very early age. Yet, if he had been given a chance, there was probably one profession he would yet have preferred – journalism, and the opportunity to be a foreign correspondent reporting world affairs. ■

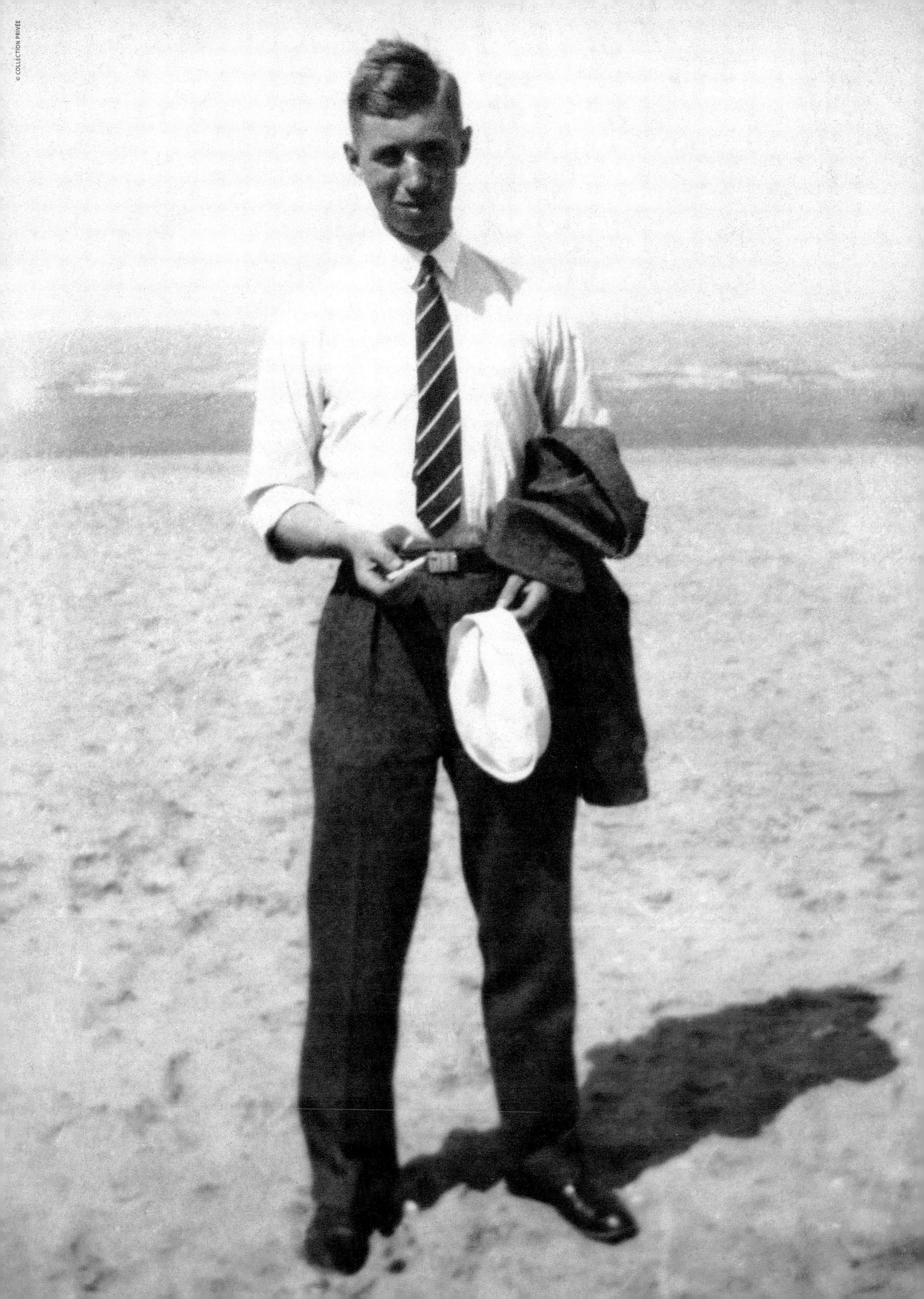

CHAPTER THREE

A journalist at heart

When as an eighteen-year-old straight out of school Georges Remi accepted his first job on the newspaper *Le Vingtième Siècle*, it was, disappointingly, not as a journalist. Despite his hopes for something more exciting, he had little choice but to accept the unglamorous position he was offered in the subscriptions department. There, starting on 1 September 1925, he began the dull daily chore of copying out the names and addresses of subscribers. It was, nevertheless, preferable in his opinion to the only other option – joining his father's boys' outfitters business.

NEW HORIZONS

Yet, even relegated to the tiny room that went with his lowly job, he had a tenuous foothold in the world of journalism. Newspaper offices, even of a Catholic journal with a limited circulation, were hives of activity, inevitably at the centre of action. With his natural powers of observation, the young Hergé could take in the myriad goings-on and learn from them. Although hugely frustrated at the unchallenging nature of his immediate work, he carried on drawing. He was contributing regularly to *Le Boy-Scout Belge* a range of drawings including his comic strip of the intrepid patrol leader Totor, precursor to Tintin. In due course his irrepressible urge to draw and his ability caught the notice of Father Norbert Wallez, the forceful cleric who was editorial director of *Le Vingtième Siècle*. Soon he found himself promoted out of the depths of subscriptions and, equipped with a camera* and a brief to draw, as well as a modest salary increase, saw his career really begin.

Although with his new responsibilities Hergé himself was by no means a reporter, he had made an important first step towards pretending to be one. Now he had to impress Father Wallez, and justify the confidence shown in him, by embellishing various sections of the newspaper with his drawings, graphic design and typography. He would provide decorative borders, title pages, plans and graphics, as well as portraits inspired by the Larousse dictionary. At a time when newspapers were less reliant on photographs, there was a whole range of possibilities of which Hergé, always encouraged by Wallez, could take advantage. On Mondays, for example, the newspaper was later to publish a special section for women readers – *Votre 'Vingtième' Madame* – for which Hergé provided elegant drawings mirroring the latest fashions.

LEFT
Hergé found himself promoted out of the depths of subscriptions, equipped with a camera and a brief to draw.

---

*There are no known examples of his photography in the pages of *Le Vingtième Siècle*, though he did experiment with photomontages in the highly up-to-date manner of Man Ray and Moholy-Nagy. It should be noted that Tintin in his first adventures sets out as a reporter armed with a camera.

Mrs Clarkson in *The Seven Crystal Balls*, Hergé's Hitchcock blonde.

ABOVE RIGHT
Hergé had an eye for female elegance. Illustration and cover for *Votre 'Vingtième' Madame*.

BELOW
Hergé and Germaine on their wedding day, 20 July 1932.

These were for the most part in the art deco manner, influenced by the fashion illustrator René Vincent, showing women of allure dressed for winter sports, boating holidays or motoring at the wheel of open tourers, neck scarves flying in the wind. Hergé had an eye for female elegance and – Bianca Castafiore, Peggy Alcazar and a selection of concierges apart – the observant reader will find that *The Adventures of Tintin* are embellished with a selection of fashionably dressed women in anonymous background roles. Then there is the pin-up of *The Adventures*, the soberly but strikingly dressed Mrs Clarkson in *The Seven Crystal Balls*, Hergé's Hitchcock blonde.

The literary supplement, *Le Vingtième Littéraire et Artistique*, which came out on Sundays, provided further fertile territory for the newspaper's young jack-of-all-trades to illustrate. Here he used a variety of styles and techniques that he felt appropriate to the subject to achieve a suitable effect. He often favoured illustrations in the manner of woodcuts which would offer a strong black-and-white contrast.

Pleased with the results, Wallez wanted to stretch Hergé further and proposed in the autumn of 1928 setting up a new supplement on Thursdays for children – *Le Petit Vingtième* – which Hergé would not only draw for but also edit. It would essentially be a one-man show. The recognition of his talent was rapid, though Wallez, later to become a controversial figure on account of his right-wing views and admiration of Mussolini[*], deserves considerable credit for promoting the young man out of the oblivion of the subscriptions department and adopting him as something of a protégé. His sponsorship of Hergé was to go as far as encouraging him to marry his secretary, Germaine Kieckens, who was a year older than the young illustrator. The friendship developed cautiously at first but was promoted by daily contact and the approval of Wallez. Attractive and forceful, Germaine was strongly protective as well as appreciative of Hergé's abilities, and the office romance flourished, even if, for a moment, Hergé hesitated while on a retreat immediately before she became his first wife.

---

[*] Wallez proudly kept a signed and personally dedicated photograph of the Italian dictator on his desk.

CHAPTER THREE **A JOURNALIST AT HEART**

Hergé had little time to trawl for fresh ideas for the new supplement. He began by illustrating a rather uninspired text provided by one of the newspaper's sports reporters: *The Extraordinary Adventure of Flup, Nénesse, Poussette and Cochonnet*. It was a haphazard tale of two 'almost 12-year-olds' Flup and Nénesse, constantly battling and bashing each other on the head with their home-made wooden swords, and Poussette, the nine-year-old sister of Nénesse, and her inflatable rubber pig Cochonnet who, deflated, slept by her bed at night. Even as children's entertainment this left a lot to be desired, but it did contain at least a couple of ingredients that Hergé could develop later. Most significantly a white fox terrier accompanies Nénesse and Poussette, while Flup, with his distinctive beret, could be adapted for one of the two comic Brussels urchins – Quick and Flupke – that Hergé was to introduce to *Le Petit Vingtième* on 23 January 1930. Flup is short for Philippe and 'ke' means little in Flemish, hence Flupke, 'little Philip'. Quick, who became the one with the beret, was the surname of a friend, Hergé was to explain later.

CELEBRATED CORRESPONDENTS...
AND TINTIN

He soon realised that the new children's supplement he was put in charge of required more than these convoluted adventures of three children and an inflatable pig. He would take Totor, the comic-strip character he had created for *Le Boy-Scout Belge*, farther and create entirely his own adventures for a new hero, to be called Tintin, an enterprising young reporter – just what Hergé, still only twenty-one, aspired to be himself. For this was the age of the grand reporter, the dashing foreign correspondent who not merely reported news from far-off corners of the globe but would often himself become the news.

In the French-speaking world at the time there were three names to conjure with and which inspired Hergé: Albert Londres, Joseph Kessel and Henri de Monfreid. In search of the exclusive reportage, these resourceful newspapermen were as much adventurers, and sometimes explorers, as reporters. They undertook long, often perilous assignments to distant destinations – by rail, steamship or flying boat – where getting their dispatches back to their newspapers was as fraught and complicated as extricating themselves from difficult situations. Enterprise and initiative were indispensable. Hazards abounded. Londres himself perished following a mysterious fire aboard the French liner *Georges-Philippar*, which sank in the Red Sea in 1932. Hergé later used press photographs of the disaster as material for *The Crab with the Golden Claws*, where he modelled the longboat used by Tintin and Captain Haddock to escape from the *Karaboudjan* on pictures of the liner's lifeboats, crammed with survivors, being buffeted by the waves.

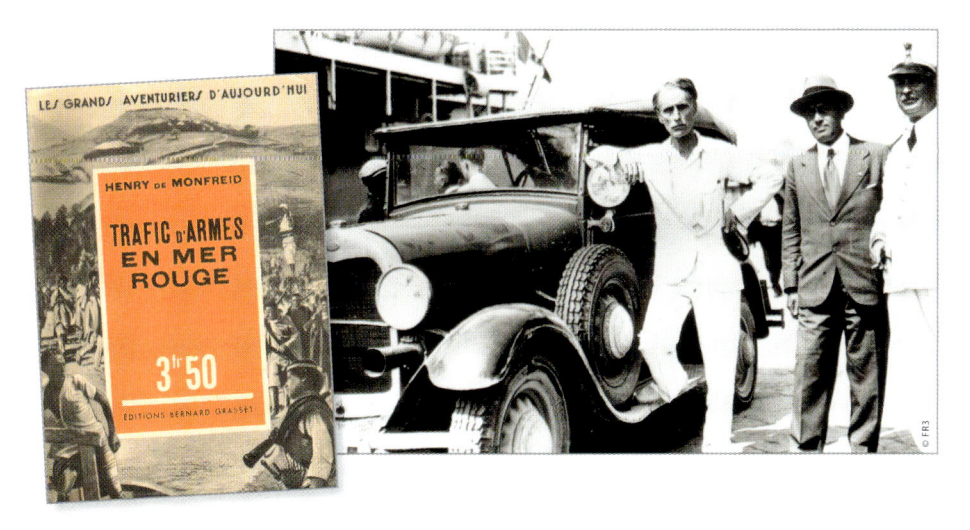

Henri de Monfreid, in search of the exclusive reportage.

Henri de Monfreid (1879–1974) expanded his exploits into best-selling novels and a very successful autobiography, *Secrets of the Red Sea* (*Les Secrets de la Mer Rouge*, published in 1932). He was an especially colourful character who tried his hand at gun-running in addition to his literary pursuits and became the model for the pipe-smoking captain – himself involved in illicit arms dealing – who rescues Tintin from his floating coffin in *Cigars of the Pharaoh*. Hergé certainly read *Secrets of the Red Sea*, for as in de Monfreid's book the captain has a store of dynamite in the hold which could *in extremis* blow the boat sky high.

In a rather charming illustration for the Flup, Nénesse, Poussette and Cochonnet saga, Hergé portrayed a cluster of reporters speaking to a pair of aviators standing by their parked aircraft. It says a great deal about contemporary journalism. While two reporters – one in a tailcoat, the other in pinstriped trousers and coat, umbrella at hand – listen to one of the airmen's account with their notebooks poised, another, more experienced it would seem, dashes off clutching his papers and hanging on to his bowler hat and umbrella, no doubt hoping to secure a scoop. Meanwhile that rarer breed at the time, a resourceful lady reporter, smartly dressed in suit and hat, is questioning the other aviator.

There were similar heroes of the press in the English-speaking world of the day. Arthur Rackham, best remembered today as a children's author and illustrator, had sent thrilling dispatches back from revolutionary Russia, from which Malcolm Muggeridge would later report[*] with distinction for the *Manchester Guardian*. Russia in the throes of Bolshevik upheaval, bordering on Europe yet distant and unfamiliar, was a particularly fruitful though dangerous destination, and it is not surprising that in January 1929 Hergé chose it for the first assignment of Tintin, described in the *Petit Vingtième* preamble as 'one of our top reporters'.

Henri de Monfreid was the model for the captain who rescues Tintin from his floating coffin in *Cigars of the Pharaoh*.

CHOICE OF DESTINATIONS

Africa too, exotic and colourful, full of natural phenomena and hazard, was another obvious choice for Tintin's second adventure, even if Hergé himself was impatient to send his newly created hero to the land of promise and native tribes, America. During the 1930s Africa was very much in the news on account of Mussolini's imperial ambitions in Abyssinia, and reporters from a variety of countries were dispatched there to unravel its mysteries, as we learn most entertainingly from Evelyn Waugh's comic novel *Scoop*.

The newsroom at *Le Vingtième Siècle*, like its counterparts across the world, would have had reports coming in from these far-flung spots, often from its own, special correspondents, sometimes generating considerable excitement with an exclusive dispatch, or scoop. This was the world from which Tintin sprang and to which he would contribute in his own exceptional way, becoming better known than any other journalist.

The pre-Tintin press gathering at the airport in the 1928 Flup, Nénesse, Poussette and Cochonnet drawing was to become a favoured device in a number of Tintin adventures. In the first two, *Tintin in the Land of the Soviets* and *Tintin in the Congo*, the young reporter is given a send-off by fellow journalists on the railway platform: in the first case by the director; in the second by colleagues, updated in the later colour edition to include portraits of Hergé himself and friends he was working with.

---

[*] At much the same time and with the same conclusions as Tintin.

CHAPTER THREE **A JOURNALIST AT HEART**

The young reporter is given a send-off by fellow journalists on the railway platform.
In the later colour edition, for which this is a drawing, Hergé includes portraits of himself (circled)
and friends he is working with.

A CORRESPONDENT IN DEMAND

In the African adventure and on other occasions, newspaper representatives queue up to compete for Tintin's reports, but he desists, insisting that he is reporting exclusively for *Le Petit Vingtième*, at least in the original black-and-white version. 'I decline: your offers remain below what *Le Petit Vingtième* is giving me and besides even if they exceeded it, I have given my word…' In the previous frame Snowy had chipped in with: 'Imagine. After reporting like ours in Russia, we can't settle for so little!' By this reckoning *Le Petit Vingtième* must have been a surprisingly generous employer. In that first edition of 1931 the sums offered by the variously suited newspaper executives were already high. By the time of the 1946 colour edition – which finally appeared in English in 2005 – the amounts had risen even further. Tintin is still in his pyjamas when there is a knock on the door and the trio of newspapermen enter his hotel room. 'Mister Tintin. I am instructed by the NEW YORK EVENING PRESS to offer you five thousand dollars for all your dispatches from Africa. Here's our cheque for a thousand to cover your preliminary expenses, and here is the contract… Please sign here…' says the cigar-chomping American.

'Mister Tintin, the LONDON DAILY, which I represent, will give you one thousand pounds sterling for exclusive rights to your account of your forthcoming adventures in Africa. I take it you agree?' adds the Englishman, who no longer wears spectacles as in the early version.

The formally attired Portuguese puts in his bid: 'And I, Senhor Tintin, represent the DIARIO DE LISBOA, of Lisbon. If your excellency would do us the honour of granting us the exclusive rights to your dispatches, we would be happy to pay you the sum of fifty thousand escudos…'

In the first black-and-white edition the Anglo-Saxons double their offers and, left behind, the Portuguese can only comment: '*C'esto tro chero por continuar!*' – It is too expensive to continue. This detail is dropped later when Tintin responds to the auction by saying: 'Gentlemen, thank you. Your offers are certainly very interesting, but I can't accept. I am already committed to other papers. I have given them an exclusive on my reports.' By then *Le Petit Vingtième*, which had launched him so successfully, no longer existed.

Newspaper representatives queue up to compete for Tintin's reports.

THE REPORTER AT WORK

Despite his acclaim as a reporter, however, we see Tintin writing a report only once, in the Soviet adventure, where, typewriter-less, he pens a dispatch of an exaggerated length no editor would care to contemplate. After repeated scrapes with thoroughly malevolent Bolsheviks, the reporter declares: 'We'll go back to the inn. I must write up my report for the paper.' He arrives at his simple but pleasantly appointed room. 'I must do a good article… I wonder if that's enough copy?' he asks hours later after completing piles of prose, written laboriously in longhand. Somehow he stuffs most of it into an envelope. 'There, that's done. But how can I get this back to the office?… Oh well, we'll think about that tomorrow. Now to bed.'

After Russia, Hergé wanted to send Tintin directly to America to report on capitalist excesses after his exposé of the harsh realities of communism. Father Wallez had other ideas, however. The Congo, Belgium's vast colony in the heart of Africa, beckoned. The Colonial Service found it difficult to recruit young Belgians as officers and administrators and Wallez felt that Tintin's example could give a welcome boost to interest in the colony. It was one of the few times Hergé bowed to editorial pressure and, as was his habit, Tintin made the news. By the time readers reached page 53 of the adventure, he was all over the local press – 'Reporter Tintin unmasks tribe of gangsters' – which is full of praise for the 'young Belgian reporter…' To ensure that Tintin's trip to America would not be subject to any further delay, Hergé made a link between the diamond production racket the reporter uncovers and Al Capone, king of the Chicago gangsters. And so it is to 'Chicago, 1931, when gangster bosses ruled the city…' that Tintin departed forthwith. An early view of Capone follows. 'Right, you guys, listen, and listen good… Tintin, world reporter number one, is coming here to clean up.' In the first black-and-white version, Capone had described Tintin as 'the famous Belgian reporter of *Le Petit Vingtième*'.

Tintin continues to make the headlines more as a crime-buster than a reporter. So by page 14, the newspaper vendors are shouting: 'CHICAGO TRIBUNE! Reporter grabs gangsters!… Sensation!… Read all about it!… Full story!… Get your Chicago Tribune here!' The adventure races on, and at the bottom of page 41 the villainous Bobby Smiles has a shock when he picks up a newspaper and reads the headline: 'FAMED BOY REPORTER CHEATS GANGLAND KILLER'.

Despite his acclaim as a reporter, however, we see Tintin writing a report only once.

At the banquet later held in his honour, the toastmaster describes him as 'a newsman as fearless as he is modest'. In three adventures serialised over three years, Hergé had created in Tintin just the hero reporter he would so much have liked to be himself. While intrepid and resourceful in the best scouting tradition, *Le Petit Vingtième*'s star reporter had all the skill, determination and news sense of Fleet Street's finest investigative journalists. He was the master of the 'on-the-spot' exclusive report that could – and in the case of *Le Vingtième Siècle* did – do so much to boost circulation. With every weekly appearance of Tintin in the children's supplement, *Le Petit Vingtième*, sales of the parent newspaper soared to new heights.

FROM NEWSPAPER TO BOOK

As the serialisation of each adventure was concluded in *Le Petit Vingtième*, Father Wallez arranged a joint venture with Hergé for it to come out in book form under the newspaper's imprint – Les Éditions du Petit 'Vingtième'. This continued for the first three adventures, with Tintin described on the cover as 'Reporter of the "Petit Vingtième"'. By the time the fourth adventure, *Cigars of the Pharaoh*, was completed, the long-established* and distinguished Tournai publisher Casterman had taken over the book production of what now became *The Adventures of Tintin, Reporter*. The reporter tag was to remain for the remainder of the black-and white editions until just before the war and *King Ottokar's Sceptre*. In *The Shooting Star*, the second of the adventures to be written during the German occupation, Tintin sets out on the expedition to locate the meteorite as 'the representative of the press'.

By now, however, Tintin had become more of a detective than a reporter. This was particularly evident from *The Secret of the Unicorn* onwards. The association with *Le Petit Vingtième* had gone – the Nazis had closed the Catholic newspaper down on occupying Brussels. His reputation, however, was made, and Tintin could continue as a freelance, appearing during the war years in Belgium's leading newspaper *Le Soir*, even if it was to bear the stigma of being sanctioned by the German occupying authorities, and afterwards in the specially created *Tintin* magazine.

Though Tintin no longer pursued his adventures so obviously as a reporter, the association was to continue to the end. In the final, unfinished adventure, *Tintin and Alph-Art*, the ill-fated art dealer Henri Fourcart wants to meet Tintin 'as he is a journalist'.

Hergé's exposure to journalism at *Le Vingtième Siècle* and subsequently gave him an insight into the profession which he was to find useful throughout *The Adventures of Tintin*, where newspapers are regularly used as tools to move the story on. A favourite device was a front page or a press review – a selection of newspaper articles arranged to record the progression of events, often at the denouement of the adventure. As already noted, this was first used in *Tintin in the Congo* and again at the end of *Cigars of the Pharaoh* and *The Blue Lotus*, as well as very effectively later for the conclusion of *The Black Island* and *The Red Sea Sharks*, tying up all the loose ends of the narrative. In *The Calculus Affair* such a press review occurs much earlier – on page 13, reporting the mysterious shattering of glass at Marlinspike – and extends to the international press. Press headlines, as seen in *Tintin in America*, are also a favoured means of propelling the story forward and continued to the end – they are much used in *Tintin and the Picaros*, and even in the unfinished *Tintin and Alph-Art*, recording the disappearance and death of the art experts. On other occasions, as at the start of *The Blue Lotus* or *The Seven Crystal Balls*, a newspaper clipping could set the scene with a résumé of preceding events.

Tintin had become more of a detective than a reporter.

OPPOSITE LEFT
At the banquet later held in his honour, the toastmaster describes him as 'a newsman as fearless as he is modest'.

OPPOSITE RIGHT
Tintin continues to make the headlines more as a crime-buster than a reporter.

---

* It was founded in the eighteenth century.

Sometimes Hergé uses reporters as participants as at the end of *The Black Island*, where they eagerly pack the quayside to greet Tintin on his return from the doom-laden isle.

CHAPTER THREE **A JOURNALIST AT HEART**

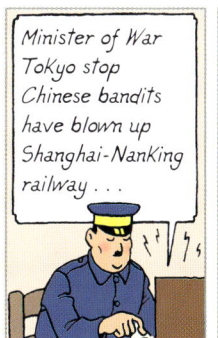

> Minister of War Tokyo stop Chinese bandits have blown up Shanghai–Nanking railway...

> Damage to property not significant Stop

> Not significant! We'll soon see about that...

> This is Radio Tokyo!... The effrontery of Chinese guerrillas knows no bounds! News just in details a treacherous attack on the Shanghai-Nanking railway...

> ...Having blown up the track, the brigands...

> ...stopped the train and attacked the innocent passengers...

RADIO AND TELEVISION

On occasions Hergé would switch to other media for the purposes of the adventure. Radio, which played an important part in *The Blue Lotus*, broadcasting across the globe the Tokyo Radio report of an attack on the Shanghai–Nanking railway, is a favourite alternative. It brings Tintin the news of the theft of the fetish from the Museum of Ethnography at the start of *The Broken Ear* and later of an eventual ceasefire between the warring forces of San Theodoros and Nuevo-Rico. Moreover, a prematurely terminated radio broadcast by Captain Haddock – overcome by a glass of water – concludes *The Crab with the Golden Claws*. Outlining or describing events, radio sets play as significant a role as newspapers in *The Adventures*, and for similar purposes.

Television reporting is also brought in, whether winding up the enigmatic ending of *Flight 714* or reporting the arrival of Bianca Castafiore in San Theodoros at the start of *Tintin and the Picaros*, and the subsequent duel of diatribes between Captain Haddock and the odious General Tapioca. It features as early as *The Black Island*, the first version of which dates from 1937, with its showing of the accidental, trophy-winning aerobatics of the Thom(p)sons. In *Tintin and Alph-Art* there is a television interview with Emir Ben Kalish Ezab – predictably disrupted by his delinquent son Abdullah – in which the oil-rich sheikh startles his interviewer by saying that on his European tour – money being no object – he would have liked to buy such European heritage landmarks as Windsor Castle, the palace at Versailles, the Eiffel Tower and, also in Paris, the Centre Pompidou. He adds that he cannot understand his offers being turned down.

Sometimes Hergé uses reporters as participants, as, for example, at the end of *The Black Island*, where they eagerly pack the quayside to greet Tintin on his return from the doom-laden isle. Then in *The Castafiore Emerald* a whole television team, as well as uninvited paparazzi, descend on Marlinspike Hall. The journalists return in force to interview Haddock over his spat with General Tapioca – and to sample his Loch Lomond whisky – in *Tintin and the Picaros*. The dress and manners of the contemporary press are caught with Hergé's customary acute observation and humour. Journalists were no longer the reporter-adventurers – on which he had modelled Tintin – of the first adventures, or the lone observer eavesdropping at the start of *Red Rackham's Treasure*, but they preferred now to hunt in a pack. It was just such an array of motley media types that was to face Hergé and Chang at their emotional reunion at Brussels' Zaventem airport in March 1981.

ABOVE
On occasions Hergé would switch to other media for the purposes of the adventure.

THE ADVENTURES OF HERGÉ, CREATOR OF TINTIN

A NATURAL JOURNALIST

Although in some respects himself an armchair reporter, or perhaps more accurately editor, sending Tintin out on far-flung and dangerous assignments while he remained cosily cocooned in Brussels, Hergé was a thoroughly professional journalist. He was diligent, conscientious in his gathering of material, hyper-observant, questioning and always balanced and fair – attributes to which all journalists should aspire. Only once did he lean too heavily on one source – Joseph Douillet's *Moscou sans voiles* (Moscow Unveiled) in the opening adventure, *Tintin in the Land of the Soviets*. It was one of the reasons he later refused to update the adventure and have it republished in anything but a facsimile of the original edition.

The views he expressed throughout *The Adventures of Tintin* were liberal, considered and convincing. The forced vote for the communist list and the earmarking of food for export while people starved at home described in the Soviet adventure were echoed in contemporary descriptions by newspaper correspondents, including Malcolm Muggeridge in the *Manchester Guardian*. The forcible eviction of the Native Americans from their ancestral lands by the National Guard following the discovery of oil, poignantly depicted in *Tintin in America*, reflected the ill treatment that persisted into the twentieth century. In the final completed adventure, *Tintin and the Picaros*, baton-wielding riot police patrol the slums at the beginning and end of the adventure despite a regime change one would have hoped was for the better. Only their uniforms have altered. A stronger condemnation of dictatorship in any form could not have been made in any newspaper editorial.

ABOVE
A stronger condemnation of dictatorship in any form could not have been made in any newspaper editorial.

RIGHT
The starving people described in the Soviet adventure were echoed in contemporary descriptions by newspaper correspondents.

FACING PAGE
Weekly children's supplement *Le Soir Jeunesse*, modelled on *Le Petit Vingtième*.

52

FAIR PLAY

It is this sense of fairness, of support for the underdog and desire for justice, felt by Hergé and championed by Tintin, which makes nonsense of his detractors' accusations that he held unsavoury right-wing views. His career may have been launched and propelled by Father Wallez, a priest with open fascist leanings, and in the Catholic-conservative circles in which he moved there were friends who were sympathetic or even supporters of the future Nazi occupiers, or members of the 'Rexist' Belgian fascist party, but Hergé was not one of them. His views are spelled out clearly in one of Tintin's finest adventures, *King Ottokar's Sceptre*, where a minor Balkan kingdom's independence is saved by the intrepid reporter from a carefully planned fascist takeover, masterminded by a certain Müsstler – a transparent amalgam of Mussolini and Hitler. It was inspired by Hitler's takeover or 'Anschluss' of Austria in March 1938, and with acute and prophetic awareness of the fragile neutrality of another small kingdom – Belgium – that was to be violated in May 1940.

Hergé knew Léon Degrelle, the Rexist leader who became a favourite protégé of Hitler, from his time as a foreign correspondent of *Le Vingtième Siècle* in strife-torn Mexico, and had even illustrated a book of his (*L'Histoire de la guerre scolaire* – The Story of the Scholastic War, published in 1932). Degrelle could even claim to have had a hand in the development of the strip cartoon, as Hergé acknowledged in an interview in the newspaper *La Libre Belgique* in December 1975. 'I discovered the strip cartoon thanks to… Léon Degrelle! He had left as a journalist for Mexico and sent back to *Le Vingtième Siècle* not only personal reports, but also local newspapers (to convey the atmosphere) in which there were American strip cartoons. That's how I came across my first comics.'

Degrelle, who survived the war and a death sentence *in absentia* afterwards to live in comfortable exile in Franco's Spain, made more of the association than there was. He, like many, was an admirer of Hergé's work, had acquired some of his drawings while at *Le Vingtième Siècle*, and when his movement was in the ascendancy offered him employment as the official Rexist illustrator. Hergé very wisely turned down the offer and there was no further association.

NOT SO WISE

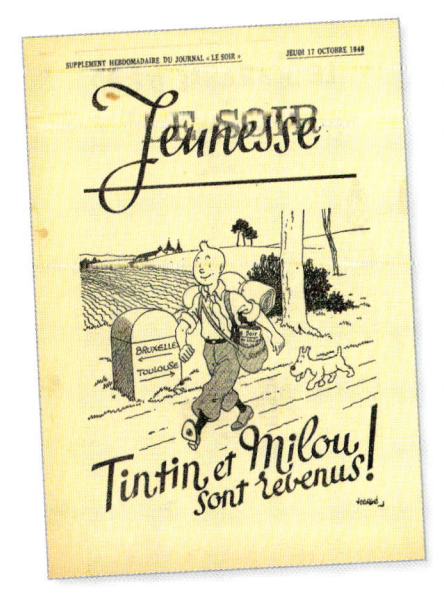

In retrospect Hergé was not so wise, however, to jump at the opportunity of taking Tintin to the much larger circulation *Le Soir*, Belgian's leading daily, when in May 1940 the German occupying authorities closed down *Le Vingtième Siècle* on the grounds that it was a Catholic newspaper. They decided to keep *Le Soir* going and use it as a propaganda organ. Disapproving Belgians came to call it '*Le Soir volé*' ('the stolen *Soir*'). At first Tintin was tucked out of harm's way in the weekly children's supplement *Le Soir Jeunesse*, modelled on *Le Petit Vingtième*, set up by Hergé a dozen years earlier. As the war continued, however, paper supplies became increasingly limited and the supplement was sacrificed. Tintin found himself moved to the news pages, which he shared most unfortunately and uncomfortably with reports of the Wehrmacht's latest successes. Hergé's acceptance of *Le Soir*'s offer of employment had resulted in Tintin, the champion of just causes, appearing on the wrong side. Hergé had exposed himself to criticism for naivety, if not sympathy for the enemy, and the moment the tanks of the British Guards' Armoured Division liberated Brussels in September 1944, he was blackballed and, like other journalists of *Le Soir*, banned from working. Some were tried and some were sentenced.

Hergé himself was detained on four occasions by various factions and spent one night sharing a prison cell with other suspected collaborators. Guilty, in his view and that of his many admirers, of nothing more than trying to divert and cheer up Belgians enduring the grim realities of occupation, Hergé was ultimately exonerated, but the experience left a bitter memory. The unfairness rankled and he suffered greatly for what may be seen as no more than an error of judgement on his part. Other artists who may also have been politically naive, such as the writer P. G. Wodehouse with his Berlin broadcasts or the conductor Wilhelm Furtwängler continuing to perform under the swastika, were to be subject to similar aspersions and damage to their reputations.

Hergé did not, moreover, help his cause by the loyalty he showed to old friends who had been more significant transgressors during the difficult years of occupation. Loyalty may have been a boy scout virtue that he espoused fully and for life, but there were times when it could be injudicious, and the aftermath of occupation, when recrimination and retribution were rife, was certainly such a period. Opponents – and there were those who were jealous of his success – mistakenly took this as sure evidence that he shared their extreme right-wing views. They evidently had not studied *The Adventures of Tintin*, where his opposition to totalitarianism and injustice is obvious from the start. Bolshevik thugs and bullies may be the targets in the first adventure, but capitalist profiteers are quickly exposed in *Tintin in America*, as well as *The Broken Ear*. Japanese militarism and imperialism are highlighted in *The Blue Lotus* in anticipation of the even worse excesses to come and, as already shown, fascist conspiracy lies at the core of *King Ottokar's Sceptre*.

Fascist conspiracy lies at the core of *King Ottokar's Sceptre*.

SUPERFICIAL CENSORSHIP

Curiously, during the occupation the German censors took exception to and banned only two of the Tintin books, *Tintin in America* and *The Black Island*, both because of their geographic settings – America and Britain – already evident on their covers. *The Black Island* additionally had as its unscrupulous villain a Dr Müller, a German spy and counterfeiter modelled on an actual Nazi whom Hergé had read about. The Tintin books that were obviously critical of German expansionism or the military ambitions of its ally Japan, however, *King Ottokar's Sceptre* and *The Blue Lotus*, escaped through the net, though Hergé was warned by an official about the wisdom of depicting a Heinkel fighter-bomber, hijacked by Tintin in the Balkan adventure. Though rattled, Hergé did not take much notice, for when he revised the adventure for the colour edition, he substituted a Messerschmitt 109 fighter, an even better-known Luftwaffe aircraft, for the Heinkel. The censor clearly did not read *The Adventures of Tintin* too closely.

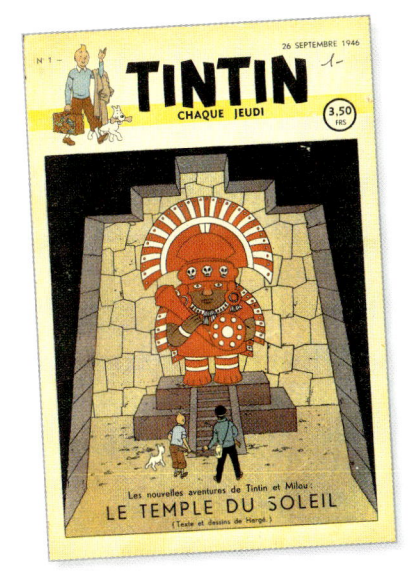

CHAPTER THREE **A JOURNALIST AT HEART**

After the war, and the tribulations that followed, Tintin was able to resume his adventures in the pages of *Tintin* magazine, a weekly specially created by the businessman Raymond Leblanc to bring the reporter back into circulation alongside work by other up-and-coming Belgian strip cartoonists. Leblanc asked 'Monsieur Hergé', as he called him, to be artistic director of the new magazine, named after his boyhood hero. Leblanc was an entrepreneur with a Midas touch who had already been captivated by Tintin's first adventures as a teenager and had made his way to Brussels from the Ardennes to welcome the reporter back from the Congo. He was exactly the right person to bring Hergé and Tintin out of the morass of post-war acrimony. He himself had an impeccable war record: a young infantry subaltern when Belgium fell, he transferred into the customs service, doubling for the resistance when off-duty.

Towards the end he turned the tables on a group of German soldiers by a daring ruse, capturing them almost single-handed, ready to be handed over to the advancing Irish Guards. He then became a liaison officer with the British forces until the close of hostilities. More than fifty years on, in 2006, at his home in Brussels, Leblanc, aged ninety-one, proudly showed me the pay-books he had 'liberated' from his German prisoners and held on to as trophies ever since.

RETURN TO JOURNALISM

So, thanks to Leblanc and *Tintin* magazine, Hergé and Tintin were able to return to journalism. Tintin, who had begun in 1929 as 'one of the top reporters' of *Le Petit Vingtième*, continued on the staff of *Le Soir* from 1940 to 1944, now in September 1946 had his own publication, even if he was only to occupy a small central part of it. His name in itself was its selling point and sales quickly reached an impressive 100,000 copies. Hergé was able to pick up the narrative of *The Seven Crystal Balls*, abruptly interrupted in September 1944, and henceforward, up to and including the final completed adventure, *Tintin and the Picaros*, each adventure appeared in the pages of *Tintin* magazine prior to its publication in book form by Casterman. Hergé had spent the two years between the suspension of *Le Soir* and the launching of *Tintin* magazine putting earlier adventures into colour, with the help of Edgar-Pierre Jacobs and Alice Devos, for their republication by Casterman in the new sixty-two-page format. For *Tintin* magazine, the adventures would unfold week by week for the first time in colour. Tintin would no longer appear initially in black and white, except for Hergé's preparatory drawings and the finished pages inked for final colouring by his assistants.

ABOVE
Thanks to Leblanc and *Tintin* magazine, Hergé and Tintin were able to return to journalism.

RIGHT
Taking on a small team Hergé created the Studios Hergé in 1950.

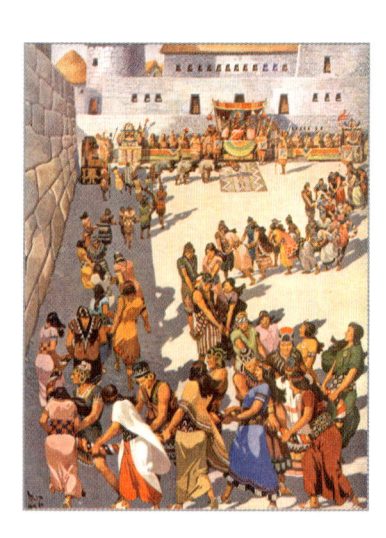

BUILDING UP AN ARCHIVE

Under these new working conditions, with the benefit of a small team that in 1950 was to become formalised as the Studios Hergé, it was back to the old routine and working practices. Hergé researched his stories as he had always done, in true journalistic fashion, by resorting to the cuttings library, an indispensable resource held by every newspaper. Already early on, Hergé had learned the fundamental value of extensive documentation, and rather than rely solely on the files held by *Le Vingtième Siècle*, he began building up his own archive, collecting all sorts of material for possible future use. There were cuttings from newspapers, magazines, journals, catalogues, postcards and a variety of ephemera that he believed might one day be of use. He constantly added material and arranged it according to his own criteria. Hergé was an early European subscriber to *The National Geographic Magazine*, which enjoyed a considerable following in the United States. He used it increasingly as a key source for subjects, settings and decor in the post-war years. *The Prisoners of the Sun*, sequel to *The Seven Crystal Balls*, was heavily dependent on the February 1938 issue of the magazine which he had set aside, with an article by Philip Ainsworth Means, 'The Incas: Empire Builders of the Andes', with twenty-six illustrations and accompanied by 'In the Realm of Sons of the Sun', ten paintings by H. M. Herget. Hergé, with his sharp sense of humour, must have been amused by the artistic contribution of his near namesake, whose material inspired several scenes in the Tintin adventure, notably the snake dance preceding the sacrifice, the procession of the virgins and the imperious High Priest himself.

A decade later, in 1956, Hergé came across a newspaper article about a 'modern-day slave trade' in which Africans wanting to make the pilgrimage to Mecca were tricked into slavery in Arab states. It became the basis for *The Red Sea Sharks*, with the added ingredient of the sensational disappearance of the British frogman Lionel 'Buster' Crabb during a visit to Portsmouth in April of that year of the Soviet warship *Ordzhonikidze*, which had brought Nikita Khrushchev, the Soviet leader, on a goodwill visit to Britain. Crabb, it seems, working for naval intelligence but without government approval, made a bungled attempt to inspect the hull of the Russian cruiser. Exactly what happened has never been disclosed by either side, but the frogman's headless body was found a year later in Chichester harbour. Identification was made on the basis of the unusual wetsuit he was wearing. Hergé was fascinated by the story

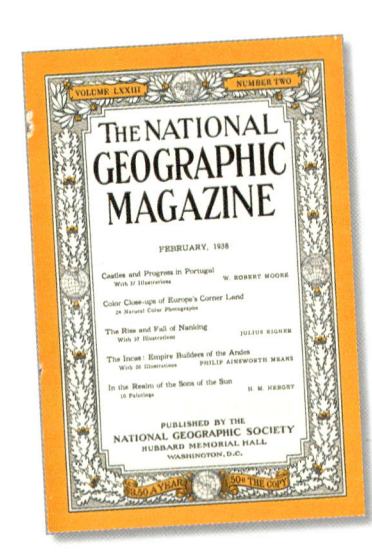

Hergé was an early European subscriber to *The National Geographic Magazine*, which enjoyed a considerable following in the United States. He used it increasingly as a key source for subjects, settings and decor.

and kept press photographs of the ill-fated Crabb that he used for the hapless frogman sent to plant a limpet mine on the hull of the *Ramona*. His attempt fails when he is struck a heavy blow on the head by the ship's anchor.

Commander Crabb had won the George Medal for his work as a wartime frogman specialising in removing German limpet mines from merchant ships. He had retained his links with the Royal Navy and intelligence services but was not a serving officer when, on 17 April, he checked into a Portsmouth hotel with a mysterious Mr Smith*, believed to be a navy liaison official from MI6, the Secret Intelligence Service. Smith and Crabb left early on 19 April and the commander was never seen alive again. Smith returned later that day, paid the bill and collected their belongings. The mystery-laden story was as gripping as a Tintin adventure.

Items gleaned from newspapers or magazines continued to inspire Hergé to the end. Two of the central ideas of his last unfinished work, *Tintin and Alph-Art*, were plucked from the glossy weekly *Paris-Match*, which he had already parodied wonderfully as *Paris-Flash* in *The Castafiore Emerald*. A colour-spread feature in the French magazine in November 1982 on the Bhagwan and his red-clothed, necklace-bearing followers was the inspiration for Endaddine Akass and his sect, while the forger Fernand Legros, who had made the headlines in *Paris-Match* and elsewhere following his trial for selling forged modern masters – the subject of the adventure – was another model for the villain, giving him his appearance.

THE ULTIMATE FOREIGN CORRESPONDENT

Hergé ended as he began, a committed and thoroughly professional journalist who yet in a career of over fifty years had never himself reported a story. He had, however, created from clumsy beginnings on one of Belgium's smaller newspapers, the Catholic Church-backed *Le Vingtième Siècle*, the world's best-known reporter, Tintin, whose adventures became known and read in more than sixty languages in every corner of the globe. Hergé, a journalist at heart and in spirit, had fashioned his proxy Tintin, and sent him out into the world as the ultimate foreign correspondent. ∎

---

* In *Land of Black Gold*, Hergé had given the alias 'Professor Smith' to the villain Dr Müller.

The world's best-known reporter, Tintin, whose adventures are known and read in more than sixty languages in every corner of the globe.

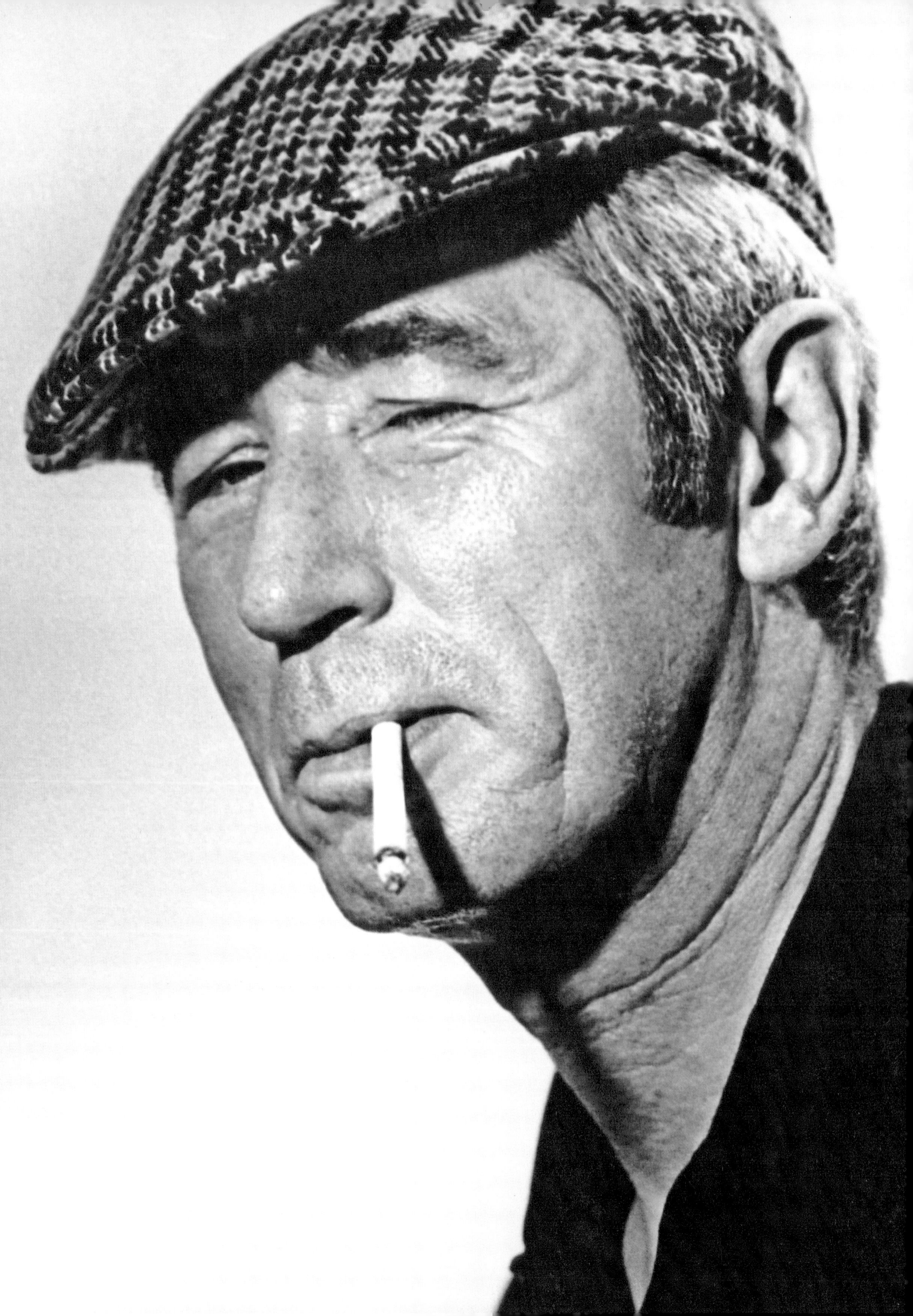

CHAPTER FOUR
The lure of the silver screen

The beginnings and early development of the cinema almost exactly mirror the evolution of the strip cartoon. For Hergé, who was quickly to establish himself as Europe's leading pioneer of the strip cartoon, to be fascinated by the silver screen and apply its lessons and examples to his own art was entirely logical. Although both art forms had their origin in the nineteenth century, they were to become two of the new arts associated with the twentieth century, seeking to entertain but reflecting at the same time much of the excitement, turbulence and drama of the times.

A LIFETIME OF CINEMA

Born in 1907, Georges Remi was ideally placed to follow the course of the cinema from the early experiments of the Lumière brothers* and the years of silence, through the introduction of sound and Technicolor, to the first successes of Steven Spielberg in the 1970s – an extraordinary breadth in one lifetime. A few months before he died in March 1983, Hergé admitted: 'I love the cinema, its language pleases me…' The very word 'cinema', according to the *Oxford English Dictionary*, dates only from 1910, when it was introduced as a shortened form of 'cinematograph', itself dating from 1896. For a child, a visit to the cinema was a most exotic and exciting form of entertainment, almost like going to the circus. To a young adult, it brought a dimension of action and romance absent from the theatre or music hall. To an aspiring artist, the cinema could provide both stimulation and ideas.

For the particular art of the strip cartoon, moreover, there seemed to be direct parallels with the cinematic techniques of shooting, cutting and framing. There can even be said to be a similar evolution, with 'talkies' superseding 'silent movies' just as speech bubbles took over from the texts above which the illustrations were previously placed in strip cartoons. Tintin first appeared in January 1929, the so-called 'year of the talkies' in the cinema. Then, during the 1940s, films graduated to colour from black and white, and so did the Tintin books. It is hardly surprising, therefore, that Hergé was a committed film enthusiast, eager to apply its lessons where possible and appropriate to his own work. This was especially true during the early years as he was developing his working methods and techniques.

Even before Tintin, the influence of the cinema is to be found in his drawings. Tintin's precursor, the boy scout patrol leader Totor, who appeared in the pages of *Le Boy-Scout Belge* from July 1926,

Even before Tintin, the influence of the cinema is to be found in his drawings.

LEFT: **Hergé in 1969.**

---

* Auguste (1862–1954) and Louis (1864–1948) Lumière were French cinema pioneers who in 1894/95 improved the cinematograph sufficiently to herald their invention of the cinema, the production and exhibition of films for public entertainment.

was, for example, presented in a cinematic manner – the masthead shows a scout* leaning against a cine camera on a tripod, with the headline 'United Rovers present an Extrasuper film: The Adventures of Totor…' or 'United Rovers present a Major Comic Film…' Sometimes the adventure would bear the credit 'Directed by Hergé' or 'Hergé moving pictures'.

Of course, this was just like the opening film credits readers would be familiar with from their visits to the cinema. It is an early example of Hergé moving with and reflecting the times. It is with the appearance of Tintin from January 1929 onwards, however, that Hergé really uses the cinema, both as a subject and as a source.

FILMS AND FILMING

When in the second Tintin adventure, *Tintin in the Congo*, the reporter sets out in his overloaded Model T Ford** (final plate of page 11 and cover of colour edition), it will be noted that he is conspicuously carrying a cine camera, which he puts to good use when he films the machinations of the villain Tom and the witch doctor. 'While I film them, my phonograph will record their voices…' Tintin says. He then improvises a cinema in one of the village huts and shows the incriminating film to the natives.

Tintin brings his cine camera and tripod out again while on safari on page 54 of the same adventure to film the maddeningly shy giraffes, and then once more on page 59 to record Snowy, emulating David's triumph over Goliath, astride the stricken buffalo.

The subsequent adventure, *Tintin in America*, has the legendary early film star Mary Pickford***, thinly veiled by Hergé as Mary Pikefort in the early black-and-white edition, sitting between a cigar-smoking general and the film mogul – on his first appearance in *The Adventures* – Roberto Rastapopoulos at the Chicago banquet given in honour of Tintin (page 57). In the later colour version (1945) the star's hairstyle is given a distinctive and contemporary Jean Harlow wave.

Readers do not have to wait long for the debut proper of Rastapopoulos, 'the millionaire film tycoon, king of Cosmos Pictures', according to Tintin. After an unhappy encounter with him aboard the cruise ship *Isis* at the start of the next adventure, *Cigars of the Pharaoh*, the reporter, with the best of intentions – seeking to rescue a damsel apparently in distress – breaks up the scene Rastapopoulos is shooting in the desert where two Arabs are horse-whipping a voluptuous blonde woman. In the early black-and-white edition the stage hero whose entrance is ruined by Tintin's clumsy intervention is unmistakably the screen idol of the day, Rudolph Valentino, while the blonde has all the allure of Pickford. In the later colour version, the actor is updated to a Kirk Douglas type while his leading lady is more Marilyn Monroe.

BELOW LEFT AND RIGHT
Tintin brings his cine camera and tripod out again while on safari to film the maddeningly shy giraffes.

BELOW CENTRE
'While I film them, my phonograph will record their voices…'

---

*   Bearing a marked resemblance to Hergé himself.
**   Between 1908 and 1927 the Ford Motor Company made 15 million of these historic cars, the first to be mass produced.
***   Pickford became the first star of the silent screen to be known by name.

CHAPTER FOUR **THE LURE OF THE SILVER SCREEN**

> STUPID FOOL!...
> BLUNDERING...
> YOU IDIOT!

RIGHT
Tintin seeking to rescue a damsel, apparently in distress, breaks up the scene Rastapopoulos is shooting in the desert.

FAR RIGHT
Material on filming from Hergé's archive.

The post-climactic moment experienced by every cinemagoer – a virtuoso touch by Hergé.

'What's going on here?' Rastapopoulos asks the director.

'Sir Galahad here has wrecked my scene!' he replies.

'By Lucifer! Unless I'm much mistaken, you're the young man I had that little tiff with aboard the "Isis".'

'Why it's Mr Rastapopoulos!'

'I'm sorry I lost my temper!' he says, shaking hands with Tintin.

'And I'm sorry if I messed up your film,' Tintin responds.

'Pah! Think nothing of it! We're making a Superscope-Magnavists feature of "Arabian Knights".'

The allusion to the cinema, and specifically to Rastapopoulos's production, continues in the next adventure, *The Blue Lotus* (1936), when Tintin, pursued by British soldiers policing Shanghai's International Settlement, ducks into a cinema to escape them. 'At least they won't come to look for us in here!'

Before the worldwide newsreel – Hergé's version of Movietone or Pathé News – Tintin and Snowy catch a trailer for Rastapopoulos's Arabian epic, posters for which can be seen outside the Shanghai cinema. Hergé conjures up atmospherically the dark but safe space of the cinema interior and, through the newsreel, its mirror of the world outside, something he was all too familiar with as a cinemagoer in Brussels. Among the newsreel items there is a reference in the early black-and-white version to Sir Malcolm Campbell's breaking of the land-speed record in his Bluebird, with 'an average speed of 445 kph'. This fascinating reference to reality – Sir Malcolm broke the land-speed record in 1935 at 301.1 mph – is cut in the slightly shortened newsreel sequence in the later colour edition.

Tintin once again visits the cinema, this time in the company of Captain Haddock, at the start of *The Red Sea Sharks*, to see a Western in which one of the actors bears a resemblance to the reporter's old South American acquaintance, General Alcazar. In the very first frame Hergé captures the audience getting up at the end of the picture, the back of their heads silhouetted against the final shot on screen of the cowboy riding into the sunset, a virtuoso effect. Again the reader feels Hergé's familiarity with that post-climactic moment experienced by every cinema-goer.

Professor Calculus experiments with colour television four years before its introduction in Europe.

That evening... Now my friends, hold your breath!... This is an historic moment!

A ROLE FOR TELEVISION

Television, so closely related to cinema, played a further role in a number of the adventures. Already in *The Black Island* (1938) – two years after the British Broadcasting Corporation's launch of the world's first regular high-definition television service – Tintin witnesses the Thom(p)sons' aerobatic antics on a television set he comes across in the forgers' lair.

In *The Castafiore Emerald* (1963) a television team with all the elaborate paraphernalia of production descends on Marlinspike Hall to interview Bianca Castafiore. Professor Calculus, meanwhile, experiments with very mixed results with colour television, four years before its introduction in Europe.

The conclusion of *Flight 714* (1968) unfolds on television with a reporter quizzing the misanthropic multi-millionaire Laszlo Carreidas, as well as Captain Skut, the Estonian pilot, Haddock, Tintin and, most memorably, Professor Calculus following their rescue from the drifting rubber dinghy. In the next adventure, *Tintin and the Picaros* (1976), television plays a key part, showing the arrival of Bianca Castafiore and her entourage in San Theodoros and their subsequent trial, as well as commercials for Loch Lomond whisky and news film of General Tapioca hurling verbal abuse at Captain Haddock and his friends at Marlinspike Hall. There is even a television set in General Alcazar's guerrilla encampment in the rainforest, adding to its surprising domesticity.

In the final unfinished adventure, *Tintin and Alph-Art*, the television at Marlinspike screens an interview with the Emir Ben Kalish Ezab, the ruler of Khemed, disrupted predictably by his impossibly spoilt son Abdullah with his bothersome bangers.

INFLUENCE, IDEAS

These are instances of Hergé using the cinema or television as a subject in itself, but even more frequent are the examples of films providing him with a source, idea or inspiration for *The Adventures of Tintin*. Already in 1929 the very first adventure, *Tintin in the Land of the Soviets*, was heavily influenced by contemporary cinema, whether the helter-skelter chases of the Keystone Kops, the deadpan acrobatic humour of Buster Keaton[*] or, more seriously, the expressionist films of a director like Fritz Lang with his dramatic emphasis on stark contrasts, strong lighting and shadows – highly effective in black and white, whether in film or for a strip cartoon. The Viennese-born Lang, famous for the Expressionist masterpiece *Metropolis* (1925), fled Nazi Germany for Hollywood after his anti-dictator *Dr Mabuse* (1933).

---

[*] A sophisticated, deadpan actor, he began his screen career as stooge to 'Fattie' Arbuckle in the Keystone Kops comedies and became one of the great silent-film comedians.

CHAPTER FOUR **THE LURE OF THE SILVER SCREEN**

Tintin in America marks a return to the fast-moving manner of contemporary cinema.

There are instances of Hergé using the cinema as a subject in itself, but even more frequent are the examples of films providing him with a source of inspiration.

Visually, the second adventure, *Tintin in the Congo*, is a gentler affair, with fewer such contrasts. Tintin is essentially on safari. Though never dull, its pace has also calmed down from the Soviet adventure. *Tintin in America*, however, marks a return to the fast-moving manner of contemporary cinema. It was awareness of film-making, and its relevance for the strip cartoon, which resulted in Hergé altering sequences to make sure that they 'read' from left to right. This was, for example, the case with the episode where Tintin bursts into Bobby Smiles' log cabin. He finds he has already gone, and in the original black-and-white edition rushes out to the left, against the flow. In the revision for the colour edition, this becomes more convincingly an exit stage right.

While the towering Chicago cityscape is directly inspired by and copied from photographs of the city he found in an edition of the magazine *Le Crapouillot* that he drew on heavily as a source, the cinema too was inspirational, notably the gangster movies that were popular at the time. Where else would Hergé have got the idea of a dummy made up as Tintin and placed in a chair being machine-gunned from an opposite window? Tintin's vertigo-inducing climb out of his Chicago hotel window is, furthermore, reminiscent of Harold Lloyd's giddy screen exploits high above street level in *High and Dizzy*.

Although Hergé's father Alexis and his uncle Léon, being identical twins, moustached and similarly dressed, were the direct model for the Thom(p)sons, it would be impossible to deny the influence of Charlie Chaplin* – or Charlot as he was known in the French-speaking world – on the bungling detectives who first appeared in *Cigars of the Pharaoh* in 1932. Hergé, according to his second wife Fanny, was a great fan of Chaplin.

He remembered being taken to the cinema by his mother as early as 1917/18 and subsequently being impressed particularly by slapstick, especially Chaplin, Harry Langdon and Buster Keaton. Stan Laurel and Oliver Hardy were also two bumbling, bowler-hatted oafs whose exploits Hergé followed in the cinema and who could bear a marked resemblance to the accident-prone detectives of the Tintin adventures.

During the 1920s and 1930s Hergé was a regular cinemagoer, even if the success of Tintin left him with less and less free time. These were the golden years of the cinema, when it superseded the theatre and music hall in popular appeal and before television offered competition. It was the prime form of entertainment, and Hergé enjoyed it immensely, relishing the comic exploits of Charlie Chaplin, Buster Keaton and Harold Lloyd (with his trademark horn-rimmed

---

* Apart from his work on Tintin, in 1930/31 Hergé created a short-lived cartoon character called Mr Mops, who bore a distinct resemblance to Chaplin.

The handcuffs are introduced with comic consequences to manacle the already inseparable Thom(p)sons to each other.

On occasions Hergé imitated Hitchcock's trademark inclusion of himself in a fleeting walk-on part as a form of signature. Thus Hergé can be spotted, hat in hand, in the Museum of Ethnography at the beginning of *The Broken Ear* (above) and as a courtier in *King Ottokar's Sceptre* (left).

spectacles) while, on a more serious note, discovering such directors as Georg Wilhelm Pabst – he was much struck by his *Threepenny Opera* of 1931 – the Irish-American John Ford, director of *Stagecoach* and one of the original creators of the Western, and the drama of the English-born Alfred Hitchcock's pre-war films, which he considered 'marvellously well made'.

A LESSON IN TECHNIQUE

Hitchcock was to be of particular importance to him for his mastery of film technique, suspense and the unexpected, as well as his pacing of the narrative, qualities that Hergé sought to emulate in *The Adventures of Tintin*. On occasions he even imitated Hitchcock's trademark inclusion of himself in a fleeting walk-on part in his films as a form of signature. Thus Hergé can be spotted, hat in hand, in the Museum of Ethnography at the beginning of *The Broken Ear*, or among the reporters seeing Tintin off at the start of the colour edition of *Tintin in the Congo*, as a courtier in *King Ottokar's Sceptre*, or as a journalist taking notes outside Marlinspike Hall on page 13 of *The Calculus Affair*, and as one of the stewards at the car rally at the end of *The Red Sea Sharks*.

Of all the Tintin adventures, it is *The Black Island* which is most directly influenced by Alfred Hitchcock. His 1935 adaptation of John Buchan's 1915 thriller *The 39 Steps* starring Robert Donat and Madeleine Carroll, with its tale of the hero Richard Hannay on the trail of a spy ring, being frantically chased from the south of England to the Scottish Highlands by both the police and the villains, is mirrored almost exactly in the Tintin adventure. Substitute Tintin for Hannay, pursued by the Thom(p)sons representing the police and pitted against a band of ruthless currency counterfeiters led by a sinister German doctor, and readers have the synopsis of the reporter's one and only adventure in Britain.

It was through Hitchcock that Hergé discovered Buchan, an author whose 'shockers', as the Scotsman liked to call them, had stylistically much in common with the pre-war Tintin adventures. Hitchcock himself was very pleased with the film, recognising that the rapid scene changes of the novel made it well suited to filming. As for Hergé, seeking at the time to apply cinematic methods and techniques to the art of the strip cartoon adventure he was developing, Hitchcock's fast-paced drama provided an inspiring model.

Furthermore, Hergé was able to pick up details from the Hitchcock film for his adventure. The handcuffs that romantically lock Robert Donat as Hannay to Madeleine Carroll are introduced with comic consequences to manacle the already inseparable Thom(p)sons to each other. Neither a leading lady nor a pair of handcuffs features in the Buchan novel. Hitchcock also uses the *Flying Scotsman* for Hannay's journey north, a detail copied by Hergé in the original black-and-white version of the adventure, although the railway has disappointingly been electrified in the later colour edition.

Like Buchan, Hergé makes more of aircraft than Hitchcock, who has only a rather bizarre-looking primitive helicopter searching for Hannay. He also installs trip wires and alarms in the grounds of the arch-villain's mansion, as in the Buchan novel.

DIFFERENT TIMES, DIFFERENT PLEASURES...

Hergé would have continued going to the cinema in the post-war years – it remained prime entertainment with television broadcasts in Belgium introduced only as late as 1953 – but as the decade advanced his attendance seems to have tailed off, and Fanny can remember only rare visits to the cinema. When they began to live together in the summer of 1960, Hergé would return home from the studios and often put on a record: jazz, of which he had long been an enthusiast – Django Reinhardt was a great favourite – or else the songs of Charles Trenet, Yves

Montand or fellow Belgian Jacques Brel. Later he particularly enjoyed the Beatles and Pink Floyd, whom he could listen to for hours. At other times he would choose classical music, which he appreciated above all, particularly Beethoven, Schubert, Chopin, Debussy and the irreverent compositions of Erik Satie, which he liked for their humour and melancholy. Towards the end of his life he would discover the jazz/classical pianist Keith Jarrett and be beguiled by his improvisations. He could not summon up such enthusiasm for opera. It was a form of musical theatre he found too improbable and would happily leave to Bianca Castafiore and her admirers, among which, like Captain Haddock, he did not number. He did admit, however, to appreciating enormously the voices of three great divas of the time: Maria Callas, Renata Tebaldi and Montserrat Caballé. Callas, and particularly her immaculate, designer-led clothes sense, as well as the notoriety of her affair with Greek shipping magnate Aristotle Onassis, became a model for Castafiore as *The Adventures of Tintin* advanced.

According to Fanny, Hergé would also enjoy settling down with a book, especially at weekends: Balzac, Charles Dickens or a volume on psychology – he was particularly interested in Jung* – or philosophy, Taoism or Zen Buddhism, all were favourite subjects. He would also spend long periods contemplating his collection of paintings. Yet, perhaps strangely for someone who followed current affairs so closely and was such a modernist, a television intruded into his domestic life only in July 1969 with the United States' *Apollo XI* mission which put Neil Armstrong and Buzz Aldrin on the moon, something Hergé was keen not to miss, having successfully landed Tintin there sixteen years earlier! That was a compelling reason for him to acquire his first television set. From then on he could watch films more comfortably at home when they were shown on television, and older films featured regularly. He could catch up on some of the later Hitchcock films that he had missed in the cinema and watch repeats of others he had seen years before. 'There are numerous films of Hitchcock that I am only discovering now thanks to television,' he told Benoît Peeters in December 1982. The video-recorder, however, had not yet become an item of household equipment.

THE CINEMA, A CONSTANT REFERENCE

Although the cinema remained a profound influence on Hergé, and notably *The Adventures of Tintin*, from the beginning to the end, references to the screen are found more frequently in his early work. Already in *Tintin in the Land of the Soviets*, the use of the rail trolley by Tintin in his desperate attempt to catch up with the train bears an obvious debt to Buster Keaton's escapades in *The General*. Twice in *Tintin in the Congo*, moreover, there are references to Keaton's film *The Navigator*, when Snowy falls down the ship's ventilator and, only a page later, when he is knocked out by the lifebelt that is thrown to him. The same film is behind an idea used later in *Red Rackham's Treasure*, when Captain Haddock is tipped upside down to drain the water from his diving suit after he has gone overboard without his helmet in his exuberance to recover more bottles of aged rum.

Tintin in America is unique among the adventures in being the only one in which an actual personage, in this case Al Capone, appears as himself, but Hergé's portrayal of the legendary gangster also bears a remarkable resemblance to the Capone-like figure played by Edward G. Robinson in *Little Caesar* in 1931.

In *Tintin in the Congo* there are references to Keaton's film *The Navigator*, for instance, when Snowy falls down the ship's ventilator.

---

* His bookshelves were lined with volumes by or about Carl G. Jung, the Swiss psychologist (1875–1961) who, like Sigmund Freud, stressed the importance of unconscious memories and early childhood experiences but rejected Freud's excessive emphasis upon the sexual instinct. Jung developed his own theory of analytical psychology. Among other works, he wrote *Modern Man in Search of a Soul* (1933), which enjoyed a prized place among Hergé's books.

It has already been noted how in the first black-and-white version of *Cigars of the Pharaoh* the actor whose entrance in Rastapopoulos's desert spectacular is ruined by Tintin's interference is modelled on the contemporary screen idol Rudolph Valentino, famed for his 'handsome lover' parts in *The Four Horsemen*, *The Sheikh* and *Blood and Sand*. In his 1922 film *The Young Rajah*, Valentino is accoutred as here in riding breeches and boots. Kirk Douglas, star of *Spartacus*, takes over the role in the later colour edition or, to use cinema terminology, 'remake'.

David W. Griffith's 1919 film *Broken Blossoms, or the Yellow Man and the Girl*, starring Lilian Gish and Richard Barthelness, would seem to have rubbed off on *The Blue Lotus* (1934), though the principal inspiration for this most sophisticated of the early Tintin adventures was the firm friendship that Hergé had struck with the Chinese art student Chang Chong-chen, which gave him an insight into the real China and not the distorted Western perception of it.

For *The Broken Ear* (1936), Hergé again had the cinema in mind, whether *The Americano* of 1916, with Douglas Fairbanks Senior, or notably Jack Conway's *Viva Villa* (1934) with Wallace Beery, of which cuttings of stills are to be found among his documents. The costumes, sombreros and firing squads are common to both, as well as the finely mustachioed figure of Pablo.

The cinema has special relevance for *The Black Island* (1938). Here the appearance of the German villain Dr Müller bears a strong resemblance to the evil Dr Moreau played by Charles Laughton in *The Island of Lost Souls* (1933). As for the fearsome gorilla Ranko, Hergé had only to think of one of the most talked-about films of the day – *King Kong* (1933). Charles Dierick, who has made a fascinating study of Hergé and the cinema, has come up with the compelling theory that *King Kong* not only inspired the gorilla of *The Black Island* but also his name, as the film was an 'RKO Production' – insert the two letters 'a' and 'n' and the result is Ranko. There may also have been an association with the British Rank film organisation, whose productions opened with the memorable striking of a giant gong by a scantily clad muscleman.

Dierick points out intriguingly, moreover, that as a youth Hergé may have been familiar with the Pathé series of Pearl White adventures, episodes dating from 1914–17 in which the heroine fights bandits and drug traffickers, climbs walls, crosses rivers and even finds herself floating in a coffin, like Tintin in *Cigars of the Pharaoh*. Perhaps these were among the early films Hergé was taken to see by his mother.

For *The Broken Ear* Hergé again had the cinema in mind… Could it be Jack Conway's *Viva Villa* with Wallace Beery?

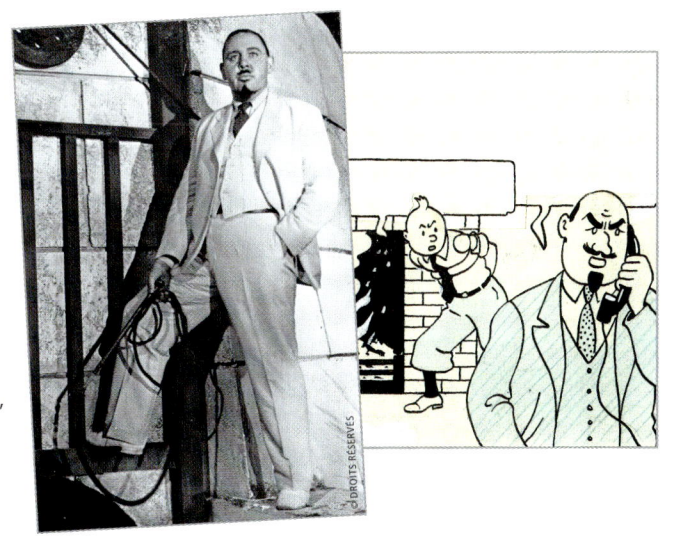

Promotional picture from *The Island of Lost Souls*, an Erle C. Kenton film of 1933, starring Charles Laughton as Dr Moreau.

The Black Island. Dr Muller in two frames of a plate published in *Le Petit Vingtième* on 22 July 1937.

In *Tintin in Tibet* the endless mountainous expanses of the Himalayas are worthy of the wide-screen cinema.

When it came to *King Ottokar's Sceptre* (1939), the atmosphere is very much that of Josef von Sternberg's *The King Steps Out*, but more specifically Hergé had in mind the 1937 film version of Anthony Hope's* romance *The Prisoner of Zenda*, starring the debonair Ronald Colman. There are parallels too in the storylines, for if Colman is not present at the wedding he cannot be king of the imaginary Balkan state of Ruritania, while in the Tintin adventure if Muskar XII appears on St Vladimir's Day without his sceptre he must renounce the throne of another fictional Balkan kingdom, Syldavia.

KEEPING IDEAS ON ICE

Hergé could remember an amusing idea for years before using it. For instance, the episode in *The Crab with the Golden Claws* (1941) when Tintin, dashing to rescue Captain Haddock, jumps into a car only for it to move backwards – pulled by a breakdown lorry (page 44) – comes straight out of Harold Lloyd's *Girl Shy* of 1923. The desert scenes of the same adventure, moreover, have a good deal of Beau Geste and the Foreign Legion films of the 1930s about them, and the retreat of the ambushing Berbers on page 38, apparently the result of Captain Haddock's extraordinary fusillade of insults, has a truly cinematic quality of composition. Similarly the endless mountainous expanses of the Himalayas portrayed with such a sense of space and depth by Hergé in *Tintin in Tibet* are vistas worthy of the wide-screen cinema or the Cinerama of the 1960s.

The films of Harold Lloyd – the first date from 1913 – that Hergé saw in his youth certainly left a lasting impression. The music-hall sequence of *The Seven Crystal Balls* recalls Lloyd's *Movie Crazy* of 1932, while the climax of the succeeding adventure, *Prisoners of the Sun*, when Professor Calculus mistakes his presence on the sacrificial pyre for part of a film spectacle, is reminiscent of the American comedian's *Why Worry?* (1923). There would seem too to be echoes of Lloyd's *I Do* of 1921 in the irrational fear displayed by Bianca Castafiore when she claims to have seen a monster at her window on page 15 of *The Castafiore Emerald*. 'But I did: I saw a monster, I tell you… A ghost or something… It was horrible… I heard a long, mournful cry, and I saw two eyes shining like diam…'

Moving on to *Tintin and the Picaros* (1976), the final completed Tintin adventure, Dierick detects the influence of Woody Allen's 1974 film *Bananas*, especially in its satirical treatment of the media and television in particular. Fanny Rodwell, however, has no recollection of him seeing the film.

Orson Welles seems furthermore to have provided at least partly the inspiration for the shady character of Endaddine Akass in the unfinished *Tintin and Alph-Art*, with his role in the 1974 film about trickery and fraud, *F for Fake*. The other model for Akass was the notorious Egyptian-French dealer in forgeries Fernand Legros, whose trial had recently made headline news.

During his last decade, Hergé's fascination for the cinema continued unabated and, as in other fields, he remained thoroughly up to date. Among the new generation of filmmakers, it was Steven Spielberg who caught his attention with his early films. Fanny remembers in particular how he was struck by his film *Duel* (1971), a 'suspense action thriller' they saw on television in which a commuter played by Dennis Weaver is pursued and terrorised by the driver of a juggernaut petrol tanker. Spielberg's *Raiders of the Lost Ark*, the first of the Indiana Jones trilogy with its distinct parallels to Tintin, came out in 1981, and *E.T.*, a supernatural subject that would have appealed to Hergé, followed in 1982, only months before he died.

LEFT
The retreat of the ambushing Berbers has a truly cinematic quality of composition.

---

* Pseudonym of British novelist Sir Anthony Hope Hawkins (1863–1933).

ABOVE
Earlier attempts to adapt Tintin for the screen, whether with actors, puppets or as animated cartoons, were remarkable only for their failure to capture either the excitement or the subtlety of the original adventures.

It was – as in the cases of Andy Warhol and Roy Lichtenstein – to be another case of transatlantic mutual admiration, for Spielberg himself became a Tintin enthusiast and was twice to negotiate for and buy the option on the film rights to Tintin, first in the 1980s and then again at the start of the twenty-first century. Although Hergé always had doubts about transferring his hero from the page to the screen, he felt by the end of his life that no one had a better chance of succeeding than Spielberg.

TINTIN IN THE CINEMA

Earlier attempts to adapt Tintin for the screen, whether with actors or as animated cartoons, were remarkable only for their failure to capture either the excitement or the subtlety of the original adventures. By comparison they were coarse and banal, and nobody was more aware of this than Hergé himself, who was careful to distance himself from them. His involvement was anyway limited, acting as an adviser where the actors were concerned and letting the studios carry out the mechanical task of animation. Others were responsible for the scenarios that were poor imitations of what Hergé himself was capable of producing for *The Adventures of Tintin*. They were proof that only Hergé could produce a Tintin adventure of the quality his readers had come to expect, and justification for the decision that the creation of new adventures should cease with his death, as he indicated himself in an interview with Numa Sadoul. 'To make Tintin live, and Haddock, Calculus, the Thom(p)sons and all the others, I believe that only I can do it: Tintin (and the others) is me… I believe that I alone can bring them to life, in the sense of giving them soul. It is a personal creation, in the same way as the work of a painter or novelist; it isn't an industry! If others were to take up Tintin, they might do him better, or perhaps less well, but one thing is for certain: they would do it differently and so, at a stroke, it would no longer be "Tintin"!'

The first attempts at animation came with the short, five-minute episodes for television based sometimes loosely on first two then a further seven of the adventures, which the Belgian company Belvision began in 1956. Belvision was specially set up for the purpose by Raymond Leblanc, founder and owner of *Tintin* magazine, which he had created after the war as a vehicle for Hergé to relaunch the dauntless reporter following the difficulties he had encountered after taking Tintin to the collaborationist newspaper *Le Soir* during the war. For all their inadequacies, the Belvision black-and-white and later colour animations nevertheless widened the audience for Tintin further, bringing new readers to the books. The English-language version that followed in the 1960s is still remembered in Britain for the booming bass voice introduction: 'Hergé's Adventures of Tintin…' It undoubtedly did something to consolidate the success of the books with an English audience. The voice was provided by Larry Harmon, an ebullient American actor who was to achieve some notoriety and popularity subsequently as Bozo the clown.

A similar function was fulfilled in the 1990s with the more sophisticated animated colour videos, later transformed into DVDs, which were produced by the French firm Ellipse and the Canadian Nelvana with the approval of the Studios Hergé. While these represented an improvement on earlier attempts at animation, they remain perhaps inevitably a pale reflection of Hergé's original creation, his own electricity of line – '*ligne claire*' (clear line), as he termed it – coming over rather stiffly in animation.

Hergé himself believed that the best chance of a successful film adaptation lay not in animation but with actors bolstered by the sort of resources available to the big-budget James Bond films. Tintin and Haddock were to him living characters, worthy of talented actors.

UNSATISFACTORY

The two Tintin films that were made during the 1960s with actors were, however, modest affairs that were singularly unambitious and left much to be desired. They could not hope to have an appeal beyond a limited francophone audience. Both suffered from the scenarios being pastiches, almost parodies of a genuine Tintin adventure. The first, *The Mystery of the Golden Fleece* (*Le Mystère de la toison d'or*), had a scenario by Rémo Forlani and was produced in 1960 in Istanbul and Greece; the second, *Tintin and the Blue Oranges* (*Tintin et les oranges bleues*), was based on a story by André Barret and was shot in Spain in 1964, including bulls, flamenco dancers, guitarists and a good sprinkling of calls of '*Olé!*' among its Spanish clichés.

For the key role of Tintin, a friend of Hergé spotted a young teacher employed as a lifeguard on the beach at Ostend, Jean-Pierre Talbot, who it was felt looked the part. Georges Wilson* played the bombastic Haddock in the first film and Jean Bouise in the second. The film producers succeeded in the difficult task of finding a fox terrier white enough to make a convincing Snowy. Following an unremarkable run in cinemas in Belgium and France, the films were turned into 'film albums' by Hergé's publisher Casterman under the title *The Adventures of Tintin at the Cinema*, which unsurprisingly failed to keep up with the actual *Adventures of Tintin* and after a while dropped out of print and view. It was proof once more that Hergé's total involvement was needed for Tintin to succeed, and neither the studios nor anyone else could offer a substitute.

Following the earlier Belvision adaptations for television, two full-length animated feature films were the next offerings for the cinema. Michel Regnier, better known under his nom de plume Greg, who was behind the Belvision television series and had become editor of *Tintin* magazine, adapted *Le Temple du soleil* (*Prisoners of the Sun*) for the big screen in 1969, amending

BELOW LEFT
Tintin et le Lac aux requins (*Tintin and the Lake of Sharks*) was not based on an adventure by Hergé but on a specially written scenario by Greg, borrowing characters and a variety of elements typical of *The Adventures of Tintin*.

BELOW RIGHT
Tintin and the Blue Oranges was based on a story by André Barret and was shot in Spain in 1964.

---
* The father of the stage and screen actor Lambert Wilson who gained an international reputation during the 1990s.

the original, adding dance scenes and introducing an Inca girl called Maita. Some three hundred people worked on the film for a year. The subtlety of the drawing in the books was lost in animation, however, and the result but a pale reflection of the original. *The Adventures of Tintin*, unlike those of Goscinny and Uderzo's rival creation Astérix, could not, it seemed, be translated satisfactorily into a full-length animated film.

This was evident again in 1972 with the next film, *Tintin et le Lac aux requins* (*Tintin and the Lake of Sharks*), which was not based on an adventure by Hergé but on a specially written scenario by Greg, borrowing characters and a variety of elements typical of *The Adventures of Tintin* – a robbery from a museum, a new invention of Professor Calculus's liable to criminal misuse, a setting in Syldavia, and Tintin pitted once more against his old enemy Roberto Rastapopoulos. Apart from familiar characters, two children – Niko and his sister Nouchka, injecting a feminine element – and their St Bernard dog, Gustav, were introduced to help Tintin come out on top. The poorly drawn and produced product, which even ends in a banal song-and-dance routine with Captain Haddock twirling uncomfortably with Castafiore, is nothing short of third rate, something that could never be said of Hergé's own work.

Casterman, Hergé's publishers, produced a book of the film the following year, confusingly formatted exactly like an actual adventure. Publishers in other countries, including Methuen in Britain, followed suit, despite the evident inferiority of a product from which Hergé's name was notably absent except for the title-page formulation 'after Hergé's characters' and 'adaptation of drawings and film dialogue: Studios Hergé'.

FINAL HOPE

The fact was that the cinema remained a greater influence on Hergé than Tintin on the cinema, which is why at the end of his life, chronically fatigued and fading away, the creator of the world's most famous reporter realised that only a film director/producer with the talent and stature of Steven Spielberg could redress the balance and bring Tintin successfully to the screen. ■

Illustration for the promotion of the animated film (1946) *The Crab with the Golden Claws*.

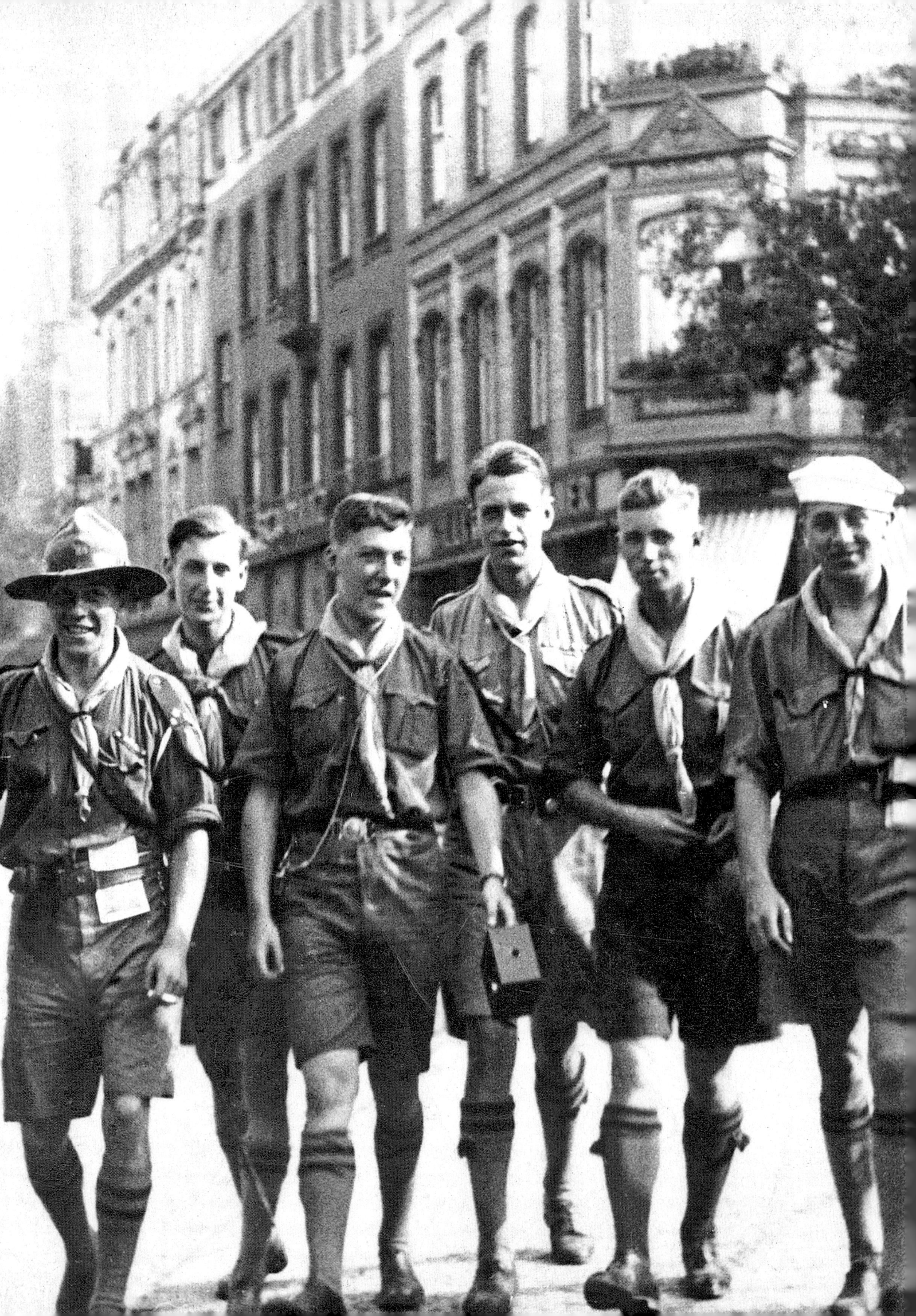

CHAPTER FIVE

Be prepared! A lifelong boy scout

If there was one thing that marked Hergé for life, it was his enthusiasm for and dedication to scouting. The values he learned as a scout stayed with him to the end and governed all his actions. Scouting brought joy to a monotonous childhood and gave him a code that he found more appealing and acceptable than the catechism of the Catholic Church. He remained true to the friends he made as a scout through thick and thin. The scouting press, moreover, gave him his first opportunities to fulfil his ambitions as an illustrator, leading to the creation of the comic-strip scout Totor, the prototype for Tintin. The famous reporter himself was a glorified boy scout, as much scout as journalist. Without Hergé's love of scouting there would have been no Tintin.

THE SCOUT MOVEMENT

Robert Stephenson Smyth Baden-Powell, founder of what swiftly became a worldwide movement, had written *Scouting for Boys* in 1908, a year after Hergé was born. Its appeal was not limited to the sons of the British Empire, though Belgium, created in 1830 with Léopold of Saxe-Coburg, widower of King George IV's daughter Princess Charlotte, as its first monarch, was very much a British-endorsed product. Born in 1857, Baden-Powell was a professional soldier who was commissioned in the Hussars in 1876. He made his name in the gallant defence of Mafeking during the South African War, becoming a national hero for holding out against the Boers with his small garrison from 12 October 1899 until 17 May 1900. News of the relief of the small town in the north-east of Cape Province sparked national rejoicing and led to the creation of a new word in the English language – to 'maffick', used to describe the extravagant behaviour of the London crowds on hearing of the lifting of the siege of Mafeking. Baden-Powell himself was invalided home, knighted in 1909 and retired from the army the following year with the rank of lieutenant-general. He then devoted his life to establishing the scouting movement throughout the world, in 1920 becoming 'World Chief Scout'. In a sideline that would have appealed to Hergé, Baden-Powell's elder sister Agnes (born 1854) was a pioneer woman balloonist and aeronaut who assisted her brother in the formation of the Girl Guides. It was all very much in the spirit of Tintin.

Belgium's amity with Britain may have dated from the marriage of Princess Charlotte to the future Léopold I, but it was much enhanced by the British fight for 'little Belgium' after its neutrality was violated by the German Kaiser in August 1914. The British and Empire sacrifice in 'Flanders fields' is unlikely to be forgotten by Belgians, who still commemorate it daily by playing 'The Last Post' at the Menin Gate memorial to the missing near Ypres. For Hergé, seven years old when the Germans with their spiked helmets (*Pickelhauben*) marched into and occupied Brussels, the impact was very immediate. Some of his early drawings were of brave British 'Tommies'. When peace came more than four years later, British ideas and institutions were highly regarded and

ABOVE
Lord Baden-Powell.

LEFT
Hergé (second from the right) with his troop, 1927.

For a young boy like Georges Remi scouting
was the principal out-of-school activity,
its camps and activities providing a healthy occupation.
It also offered many their first taste of foreign travel.

TOP
Hergé with his troop in the Alps during a summer camp, 1922.
ABOVE LEFT
Hergé with his troop and plenty of game.
ABOVE RIGHT
Hergé (right) with members of his troop.

Postcard to a friend during a camp in the Pyrenees, September 1923.

A SCHOOL OF FRIENDSHIP

Loyalty, resourcefulness and an unequivocal duty to help others became the very ethos of both Hergé and Tintin.

in the ascendant, and Baden-Powell's Boy Scout movement, which had already established a foothold before the war, gained universal appeal.

For a young boy like Georges Remi, aged eleven and a half at the end of the First World War, scouting was the principal out-of-school activity, its camps and activities providing a healthy occupation, particularly during the long summer holidays. As well as camping and other outside pursuits, the scouting bodies organised sporting competitions and events, and offered many, including Georges, their first taste of foreign travel.

Summer expeditions took him across the Alps, through Switzerland and the Tyrol to Italy, and across the Pyrenees from France to Spain. Switzerland, with its lakes and dramatic mountains, was to remain a favourite destination and refuge for the rest of his life. Fanny recalls how on their regular visits there they would hike all day long, stopping only for lunch at a simple inn or else to enjoy a picnic they had brought along. Hergé would carry a wineskin filled with the local wine. They had a particularly happy holiday in the early 1970s when they joined in the grape harvest in the Valais. The love of walking great distances dated from those scouting expeditions of his boyhood.

Scouting taught camaraderie and above all loyalty, which was Hergé and Tintin's hallmark virtue. It was this sense of loyalty which made it so difficult for Hergé to leave his first wife Germaine after years of marriage, even if, on his part, the marriage had long gone cold. Even after their separation and eventual divorce he would continue to maintain friendly relations and see her every Monday. It was the same virtue which Tintin displays heroically – and his friends think foolishly – in *Tintin in Tibet*, when, certain that somehow his friend Chang has survived the air crash in the Himalayas, he persists and risks all to rescue him. Also in *Tibet*, when it seems that both must die on the mountain face, Captain Haddock insists on making the ultimate sacrifice and cutting the rope to save Tintin, until his frozen fingers clumsily drop the clasp knife. It is no wonder that this adventure, reflecting as it did Hergé's own personal crisis, was to be his favourite among the Tintin books.

In an interview in the French daily *Le Monde* in February 1973 he noted: 'Scouting gave me a taste of friendship, love of nature, animals, games. It is a good school. All the better if Tintin bears the hallmark…'

Loyalty, resourcefulness and an unequivocal duty to help others – a good turn a day – became the very ethos of both Hergé and Tintin. Fanny recalls two incidents in particular when Hergé's scout instinct could not be repressed. On one occasion he saw a father strike a child in the street and immediately stopped to intervene in its defence, an episode strongly reminiscent of Tintin's pushing aside of the bully – 'Brute!… Aren't you ashamed?… Bullying a child like that?' – who deliberately upsets Zorrino's basket of oranges in *The Prisoners of the Sun*. On another occasion, Hergé stopped his car to pick up and help a drunken tramp who was lying in the gutter, much as Captain Haddock tries to alleviate the suffering of the 'down-and-out' he finds at the airport terminal in *Flight 714*, little realising that it is in fact the billionaire Laszlo Carreidas. *The Adventures of Tintin* are, of course, full of examples of good turns by Tintin, always on the side of the underdog, and Haddock, who, like Hergé himself, has a markedly charitable disposition demonstrated not least by his support and defence of the gypsies in *The Castafiore Emerald*.

As an eleven-year-old, Georges Remi joined the unaffiliated Scouts of Belgium, who followed closely the tenets of Baden-Powell. With them he learned the skills of knot-tying, tracking and

René Weverbergh, responsible for the Brussels district of the Belgian Catholic Scouts.

With the St Boniface troop, on its sixth anniversary. Hergé is second from the right in the second row.

fieldcraft. His move in 1920 to St Boniface's, a Catholic school in the Ixelles district of Brussels, however, led to his switching the following year to the school scout troop, which had been set up in 1919. It formed part of the Federation of Belgian Catholic Scouts and had a clear religious direction. Hergé's father is said to have come under pressure from associates to move his son from the secular to the church-affiliated scouts.

FIRST PUBLICATIONS

At first it was a difficult step for Georges as he left behind a good many friends. The St Boniface troop was both welcoming and dynamic, however – with an emphasis on social work – and he quickly struck new and lasting friendships, including with Pierre Delville, the leader of the 'Eagles' patrol into which Remi was admitted. It was Delville who was to introduce him to the English comic strip *Tiger Tim*, one of the possible influences on the later creation of Tintin. Apart from his perfect knowledge of scouting techniques, honed with the Scouts of Belgium, he quickly impressed with his drawing skills, a talent that the St Boniface scouts would use for their magazine *Jamais Assez* (Never Enough). Then, early in 1923, René Weverbergh, who was responsible for the Brussels district of the Belgian Catholic Scouts, asked Georges to illustrate *Le Boy-Scout*, which the federation published monthly. Already during the previous year, the magazine had used some of his work. For the first time his drawings would appear properly in print.

By 1927 a convergence was developing between the Belgian Catholic Scouts and the Baden-Powell Belgian Boy and Sea Scouts which during the course of the year led to their merger as the Baden-Powell Belgian Boy-Scouts – Federation of Belgian Catholic Scouting. Their two publications – *Le Boy-Scout*, for which Hergé had provided illustrations since 1922, and *Le Scout Belge* – became *Le Boy-Scout Belge*, to which Hergé would in due course bring Totor and much else. It was from its start the principal platform for his work before his promotion at *Le Vingtième Siècle* and a snowballing of demand for his drawings from all sections of the newspaper, the scouting and Catholic press, as well as advertising commissions. His tremendous versatility as an illustrator was appreciated by all.

Le Boy-Scout Belge, January 1928.

It was through his first work for scouting publications that he came across Pierre Ickx, who was very well connected in the scouting and Catholic press and gave him valuable advice and assistance at the start of his career. Already in 1923 the scouting authorities had put Ickx in charge of the Fleur de Lys Art Studio to promote and encourage art among scouts, and Georges Remi quickly became a protégé. Scouting was to give Hergé, as he soon became*, an entrée into the world of illustration that he was able to capitalise on at *Le Vingtième Siècle*.

SCOUTING TRACKS

It is not surprising that with Hergé's dedication to scouting, the movement's skills, as well as its spirit, should permeate *The Adventures of Tintin*. Only a former boy scout could have fashioned with just a penknife a new propeller blade from a tree he has cut down, as Tintin does in his Soviet adventure of 1929, or the wooden trumpet the reporter carves – again using a knife – in *Cigars of the Pharaoh* so as to communicate with the friendly elephant. But beyond such examples, Hergé extends his tribute to scouting by on occasions actually including uniformed scouts – and sometimes wolf cubs, the junior branch – in the adventures. So there are scouts among the throng greeting Tintin on his return from the Soviet Union to the Gare du Nord in Brussels, as there were in reality when the event was successfully staged as a stunt at the close of the adventure. A cub and scout are back on the railway platform to see Tintin off on the first stage of his trip to the Congo, in both the original black-and-white and subsequent colour versions. The reporter himself even wears a scout uniform, and gives the familiar salute, for the 'Tintin-Scouting' section of *Tintin* magazine in 1946.

Among the very first drawings Hergé did for *Le Boy-Scout* as early as 1922 are a set illustrating the technique of the lasso, a noosed rope used for catching cattle: the noose being thrown so as to fall over the animal's head or catch its feet. He was able to use these in the third adventure, *Tintin in America*, which dates from 1931. There, Tintin chases the villain Bobby Smiles on horseback and tries, with a singular lack of success, to lasso him. 'You can't escape, my friend! I'll truss you up like a turkey!' He proceeds to fling the noosed rope, but, as Snowy observes: 'Tintin! Watch out! You've roped your own horse!' and the reporter ends up well and truly trussed himself.

It was scouting, moreover, which awoke the deep and lifelong interest Hergé held in the North American native tribes. Many of the scouting activities, such as fieldcraft and tracking, hunting for food, the adoption of animal names, camping in tents and the almost ritual assembly around the campfire had parallels with the life and customs of the Native Americans. Scouting enthusiasts were understandably fascinated by the skills and proximity to nature, the wisdom and nobility displayed by the tribes tragically driven from their ancestral lands by avaricious exploiters. It is a subject that Hergé was able to tackle in *Tintin in America*. He may in this early adventure have portrayed the Native Americans as gullible and naive – to his later regret – but he also created one of the most poignant and political scenes in all his work when the capitalist developers drive them off their land so as to grab their oil.

---

* It was in December 1924 in *Le Boy-Scout* – under the column heading 'Wolf Cub Corner' – that he first used the nom de plume Hergé, derived from the French pronunciation of his initials reversed – R.G. From that moment on he would sign his work 'Hergé'. While his friends continued, of course, to call him Georges, the fame that came with Tintin led to him becoming better known as Hergé than as Georges Remi. He could later, if he was lucky, enjoy a degree of much-desired anonymity under his real name. Raymond Leblanc, who set up *Tintin* magazine in September 1946 as a new vehicle for the publication of the adventures, recalls how at his first meeting and subsequently he would quite naturally call him 'Monsieur Hergé'. From an artistic point of view, moreover, it had a catchy ring. The Russian artist Romain de Tirtoff (1892–1990), whose flamboyant art deco fashion designs enjoyed a considerable vogue during the 1920s, was, in a relevant example, well known as Erté, again the French pronunciation of his initials R.T. Erté gained his first significant contract with *Harper's Bazaar* magazine in 1915, and his delicate figures and sophisticated, glamorous designs would have been familiar to Hergé, who was to illustrate women's fashions himself. It is quite possible that he provided the inspiration for the young Belgian artist's nom de plume.

EXPLOITATION

It all begins when Tintin inadvertently unplugs an oil well. 'Great snakes!… OIL! A liquid fortune and no one to harness it!' he declares at the top of page 29. But already in the next frame, less than ten minutes later, according to Tintin, the first of the oilmen appears. 'OK, son! Here's the contract. Sign there! Five thousand dollars for your oil well…' But as on other occasions when newspaper executives bid for Tintin's reports, he is only the first of a number and the offers escalate up to 'a hundred grand!!!!' until Tintin replies: 'I'm terribly sorry, gentlemen, but that oil well isn't mine to sell. It belongs to the Blackfoot Indians who live in this part of the country…'

'Why didn't you say that before?' says one of the bidders sourly, while the first one on the scene finds the tribal chief, hands him a bill and commands: 'Here Hiawatha! Twenty-five dollars and half an hour to pack your bags and quit the territory!' The bewildered chief can only reply: 'Has Paleface gone mad?' In the next frame the Native Americans, children crying, are driven off their land at bayonet point by the National Guard. Three frames later, at the bottom of the page, a completely new city has sprung up. The whole episode, from start to finish, has been encapsulated remarkably in one page, one of the finest and most politically charged Hergé ever created.

ABOVE LEFT
A virulent example of colonialist attitudes is the racist abuse let off by Gibbons when he walks into the path of the Chinese rickshaw driver.

ABOVE RIGHT
Le Petit Vingtième, 13 September 1934.

This savage condemnation of heartless capitalism in America was the long-planned pendant to his indictment of communist cruelty in *Tintin in the Land of the Soviets*, and notably the scene where the starving children are given a quarter-loaf of bread only if they are 'good communists'. The commissar is distributing bread to the abandoned children. 'Communist? You're a communist?… Yes?… Bread for you…' he says, patting the boy on the head. He questions the next in the queue: 'Communist?… No?… That's what you get!… Dog!' and kicks him into the gutter.

It is strong comment and continues where necessary throughout *The Adventures of Tintin*. The racist abuse let off by Gibbons when he walks into the path of the Chinese rickshaw driver in *The Blue Lotus* is a virulent example for Hergé of colonialist attitudes. 'Dirty little Chinaman! … To barge into a white man!' the odious Gibbons shouts as he lays into the driver with his walking stick. Tintin jumps out and snaps the stick in two: 'Brute! Your conduct is disgraceful, sir!' To which the ranting Gibbons bellows in response: 'Stop me punishing a useless native, would you?… Interfering brat!' before storming to his club. There he relates the incident to his fellow club members: '…Trying to stop me beating a native… Intolerable! What's the world coming to? Can't we even teach that yellow rabble to mind their manners now? It's up to us to civilise the savages! We soon won't have any control at all… and look what we've done for them, all the benefits… of our superb western civilisation…' Then, with an expansive hand gesture, he manages to knock the drinks tray from the Chinese waiter's grip: 'You did that on purpose, yellow scum!… I'll teach you respect for your betters!' and punches the poor Chinaman on the chin. It is abominable behaviour, and Hergé was aware that it existed at the time.

Much later, in *Tintin and the Picaros*, Hergé condemns dictatorships of any political hue when he pointedly shows riot police patrolling the slums both before and after the revolution Tintin has facilitated – only their uniforms have changed. The Boy Scout in Hergé, and Tintin, can clearly distinguish between right and wrong. One of the principal purposes of Baden-Powell's expansion of the Boy Scouts into a worldwide movement was to promote international and cross-cultural understanding, all the more so after the horrors of the First World War. In their distinctive way these were objectives achieved by Hergé in *The Adventures of Tintin*, which, by the twenty-first century, were read in more than sixty languages in every continent by a great diversity of races. Like scouting, they were, nobody could really dispute, not only fun but also a force for good.

LEFT
The Native Americans, children crying, are driven off their land at bayonet point by the National Guard.

Father Gall.

Hergé (first on the left), feathered and wrapped up in a blanket, entering fully into the spirit of the fantasy…
At a scout camp in the Ardennes, 1922.

THE NATIVE AMERICANS

During the 1920s in some circles there was, again provoked by the industrial and increasingly mechanised carnage of the world war, a move back to nature in various forms. Scouting was one, as was a reassessment of the fate and customs of the Native Americans.

At a scout camp at Botassart in the Ardennes in 1922, members of Hergé's patrol, the Eagles, dressed up as Native Americans. A photograph exists of Hergé, feathered and wrapped up in a blanket, entering fully into the spirit of the fantasy. Subsequently he could recall: 'I was a "Redskin" at the moment when the scouts took as their model the North American Indians. And ever since I was interested in these people.'

The enthusiasm could be taken to extremes, and Hergé was later introduced to and struck a rapport with Father Gall, a Cistercian monk who went as far as dressing up and living as a Native American in the middle of Belgium. In 1926 he had entered the Trappist community at Scourmont, near Chimay, famous for the high-strength beer produced by the monks. Despite never having set foot in America, Gall yet learned the Sioux language so that he could communicate with them by letter. He was given the name 'Lakota Ishnala', meaning 'Lonely Sioux'. The monk collected Sioux artefacts and items of dress which he would wear with pride and dedication, meditating as he smoked a peace pipe. He was – not surprisingly – considered a leading European expert on the Native American tribes, and Hergé, seeking, as was his manner, to be as accurate in his depiction as possible, went to Father Gall for advice. For this reason the details of native dress and life are remarkably exact, unlike the cliché-ridden picture then being created by Hollywood and the increasingly popular Westerns.

When Hergé met Father Gall at Scourmont in 1948 he felt more comfortable with him than with the religious rites and regime of the Cistercian monastery. The monk had his den at the top of a small tower, a round room – 'like a Sioux tent', Hergé told his wife Germaine – reminiscent of a wigwam, decorated with eagle-feather headdresses, bows, arrows, tomahawks, guns and peace pipes. The two enthusiasts talked of the history of the Native Americans, their battles and their warriors. The next day Gall, dressed from head to foot as a Sioux chieftain – he was an honorary member of the tribe – took Hergé into the nearby woods which he considered his 'reservation' and they smoked the peace pipe according to the strict rules laid down by the tribespeople. Father Gall spoke of the native desire to communicate with all beings of the universe and the feeling for harmony with nature. He also corrected a number of inaccuracies perpetrated by the Boy Scout interpretation of Indian lore.

INADEQUACY

Hergé's impatience to include Native Americans in a Tintin adventure – his scout creation Totor had already encountered them – was probably the reason for his subsequent feeling that he did not really do them justice and argue their case as successfully as he did for the Chinese in the slightly later *The Blue Lotus* (begun in 1934). *Tintin in America* (1932) was still an early, exploratory work, and while it was brimming over with innovatory ideas presented at a rattling pace, Hergé's tight deadlines and considerable workload meant that it was also somewhat hurried. As a result the Native Americans provide local colour but little more in what amounts to only a passing episode, and twenty-five years later Hergé considered returning to the subject to treat it in greater depth. As background and at his request, Father Gall provided him with six closely written pages of text covering many aspects of Native American life and history and providing a mine of information, right up to the fact that Native Americans were among the first wave of American troops ashore in the D-Day Normandy landings on 6 June 1944. The projected new adventure would have centred on Tintin defending them and their land from exploitation by oil speculators and developers in an elaboration of the *Tintin in America* theme. It was not, however, to be. Instead, Hergé turned to Tibet.

While there were few corners of the globe that Tintin did not reach during the course of his twenty-four adventures, there were regions to which he did return and for which he seemed to have a special affinity – the Middle East and the Arab world, and South America. North America remained a one-off, and so did the Native Americans for whom he felt such sympathy.

Hergé's only compensation was to go himself with Fanny to the reservation at Pine Ridge much later, in 1971. He took an introduction to the Oglala Sioux from the redoubtable Father Gall, still, in the face of advancing years, pursuing his passion for all things relating to Native Americans. Finding them exploited and corrupted by modern American life, it was, however, a deeply depressing experience for Hergé, dismantling many of the romantic notions he had held since childhood about this once proud race.

NATIVE AMERICANS AGAIN AND GYPSIES...

Prodded by Father Gall, Hergé had eight years earlier – in 1963 – become involved in one other Native American story, the case of Ronald Newman, a tribesman from North Dakota serving in the US Army, who was sentenced by a military court in Munich to twenty years' hard labour for desertion from his unit in West Germany. Newman was homesick and had gone absent without leave. Two weeks later he returned to his barracks and was placed under arrest. Shocked at the severity of the punishment, Hergé undertook, as he said Tintin would have done, to intervene

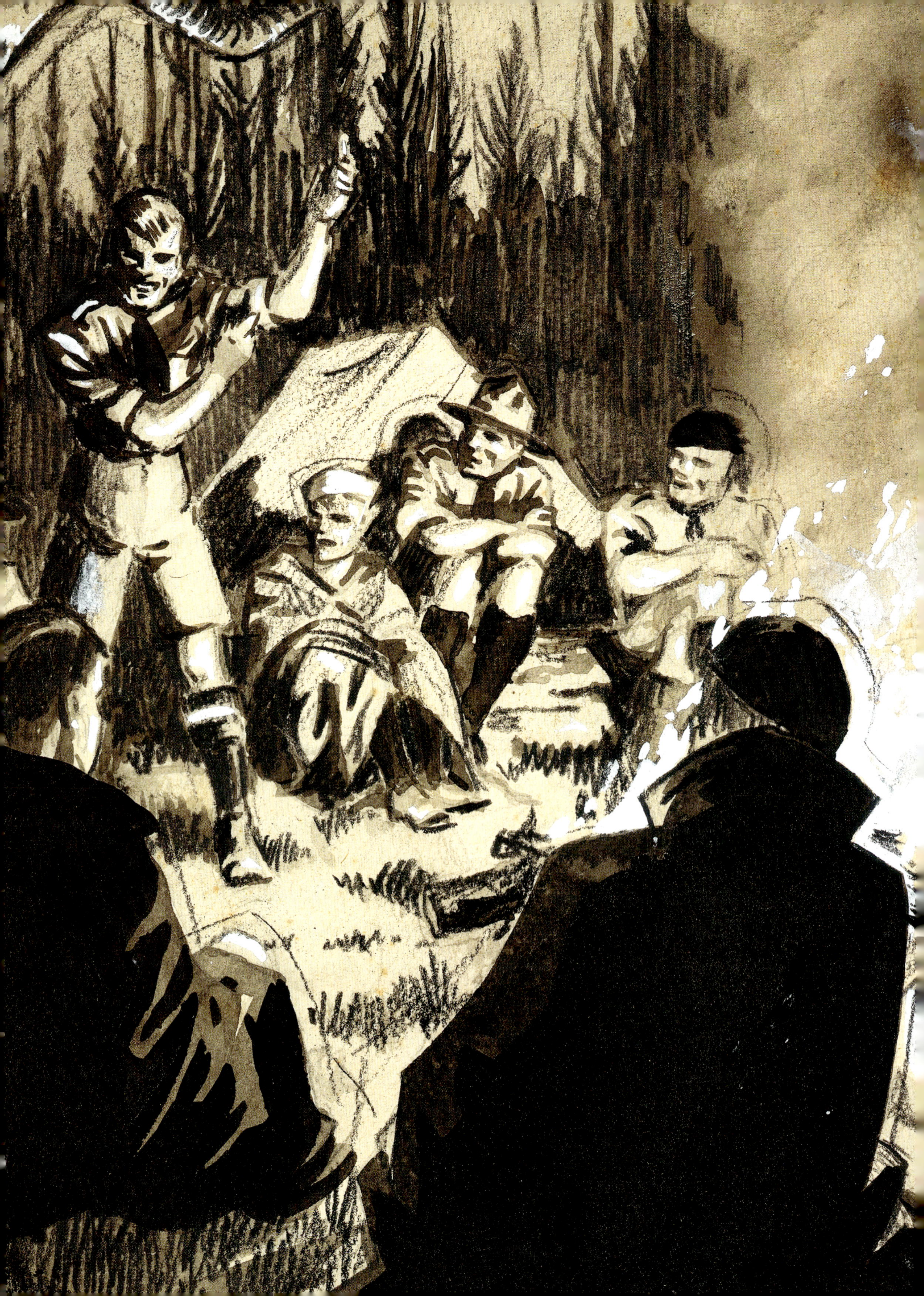

CHAPTER FIVE **BE PREPARED! A LIFELONG BOY SCOUT**

on his behalf and, for what it was worth, he wrote to General Lyman Lemnitzer, the commander of NATO forces in Europe. Even though Tintin and his friends had already landed successfully on the Moon – ten years earlier, in 1953 – beating the American astronaut Neil Armstrong by some sixteen years, the young reporter had yet to achieve the fame he enjoyed in Europe across the Atlantic. In his letter, Hergé told General Lemnitzer about Tintin, how he was 'a courageous and generous young man whose object in life was to fight against injustice and to champion the oppressed', and why he would have sprung to the defence of the young Native American serviceman. He accompanied his letter with a selection of Tintin books, pointing out that they invariably had happy endings and that he hoped this case would too. He did not expect his petition to succeed but he felt quite convinced, with his scout upbringing, that it was necessary. Of course, Hergé was not alone in lobbying on Newman's behalf, but within days of sending his missive the soldier was freed.

Gypsies were another minority group for which Hergé had understanding, again on account of his time as a Boy Scout. The itinerant life, so hard to comprehend for the settled middle class, was less remote to the scout, with his enthusiasm for hiking, camping and living off the land. The campfire in particular had deep significance for both scout and gypsy, something appreciated by Hergé. Some of his most atmospheric drawings for scouting newspapers had been campfire scenes, and the same is true of the magical moment on page 40 of *The Castafiore Emerald* where Mike (Matteo in the original French version) strums his guitar to the other gypsies congregated around the fire, its glowing embers illuminating them in a warm red light. From early on, Hergé was particularly talented at depicting nocturnal scenes, possessing a strong grasp of chiaroscuro, light and shade, and they account for some of the most poetic images in *The Adventures of Tintin*.

From early on, Hergé was particularly talented at depicting nocturnal scenes, possessing a strong grasp of chiaroscuro, light and shade.

LEFT
Illustration for *Le Boy-Scout Belge*, June 1929.

RIGHT
Frame taken from page 40 of *The Castafiore Emerald*.

Hergé, and his occasional alter ego Haddock, as well as Tintin, had a strong empathy for the often misunderstood gypsies, which is why early in the adventure the captain invites them to camp in the more salubrious grounds of Marlinspike Hall rather than near the municipal rubbish dump. 'Blistering barnacles! Now, just you listen to me,' Haddock tells the old gypsy. 'You're not staying here!… There's a large meadow near the Hall, beside a stream. You can move in whenever you like.'

The offer certainly takes one character by surprise. Nestor, the normally unflappable butler, cannot believe his eyes when he opens the door and sees the gypsy caravan. He rushes to his master. 'Oh sir!… In the drive… a whole horde of gipsies!… They say you told them to come, sir… you invited them to camp in the grounds.'

'That's right, Nestor. Show them into the big meadow, down by the stream.'

The prejudice against the travellers is, however, great. First Nestor calls them 'nothing but a bunch of thieving rogues' and warns of trouble, a view endorsed by the police inspector, and when Castafiore's jewels later go missing, the Thom(p)sons, detectives of notorious incompetence, immediately – and, of course, falsely – point the finger at the gypsies when they learn of their nearby encampment.

Then the gypsies themselves can be resentful and suspicious of the charity shown them, as exemplified by the embittered Mike. 'I hate them, the gajos. They pretend to help, but in their hearts they despise us…'

Hergé's sympathy for the plight of gypsies resulted in a sensitive and fair presentation, and one that was woven with relevance and skill into the plot. It was mature and considered, the sort of treatment he would have liked to give to Native Americans a second time around. As usual, Hergé had kept photographs and documents that ensured an accurate and sometimes poetic portrayal of the Romany families. His wonderfully rustic depiction (page 47) of the departing caravans, for instance, can be matched exactly to a photograph he had set aside. He also had useful material for the campfire scene.

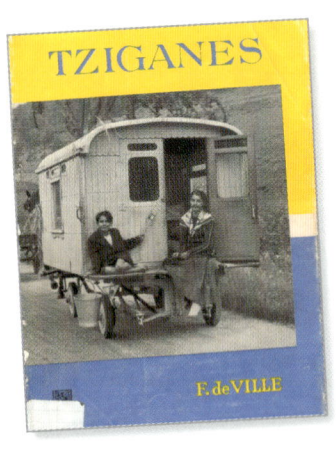

The book *Tziganes*, from which Hergé derived inspiration.

As usual, Hergé kept photographs and documents that ensured an accurate and sometimes poetic portrayal of the Romany families.

CHAPTER FIVE **BE PREPARED! A LIFELONG BOY SCOUT**

Hergé (left in the water)
was a master of improvisation,
a strong swimmer,
a proficient rock climber.

SCOUTING SKILLS

The Boy Scout motto – 'Be Prepared!' – was enthusiastically adopted by the young reporter from the moment he set out from that station in Brussels on 10 January 1929. It was Tintin's watchword throughout the adventures, and enabled him to overcome all kinds of villainy, often using skills he must have learned from his presumed apprenticeship as a scout. He knew how to breathe underwater using a broken reed, he was familiar with Morse code, could burn with a magnifying glass, signal with a pocket mirror, build a raft, skin a wild animal, and remembered his nature notes on the habits of birds. He was a master of improvisation, a strong swimmer, a proficient rock climber; he could shin up a tree with ease, tie every kind of knot, kindle a fire, administer first aid and strip and reassemble a motor car, attributes more typical of the scout than the reporter. They were to prove invaluable during his invariably hazardous assignments.

Though practical and well trained in a number of scouting skills, for which he earned his badges, Hergé himself was not quite so adept. He remembered how to put up a tent, retained a love of nature, could walk great distances and was a keen swimmer. In the Bahamas in 1972 he took to scuba diving. His love of fast and elegant motor cars, notably the Italian Lancia, which he featured in the hands of the motoring virtuoso Arturo Benedetto Cartoffeli in *The Calculus Affair*, did give him some knowledge of the complexity of car engines. He did not, however, allow precious time to be taken up by mundane activities, and his friend Guy Dessicy recalled how the day he saw him cleaning and polishing his Lancia himself he knew that something was wrong, that Hergé was going through one of his depressive spells.

From the day in 1919 when Georges Remi proudly enrolled as a Boy Scout the lessons, skills and above all the code he learned remained with him to the end of his life, to be perpetuated afterwards by Tintin. Once a scout, always a scout. The Hergé and Tintin we know would not have been the same without scouting and the tenets of its founder, Robert Baden-Powell, the hero of Mafeking, which inspired them so. ■

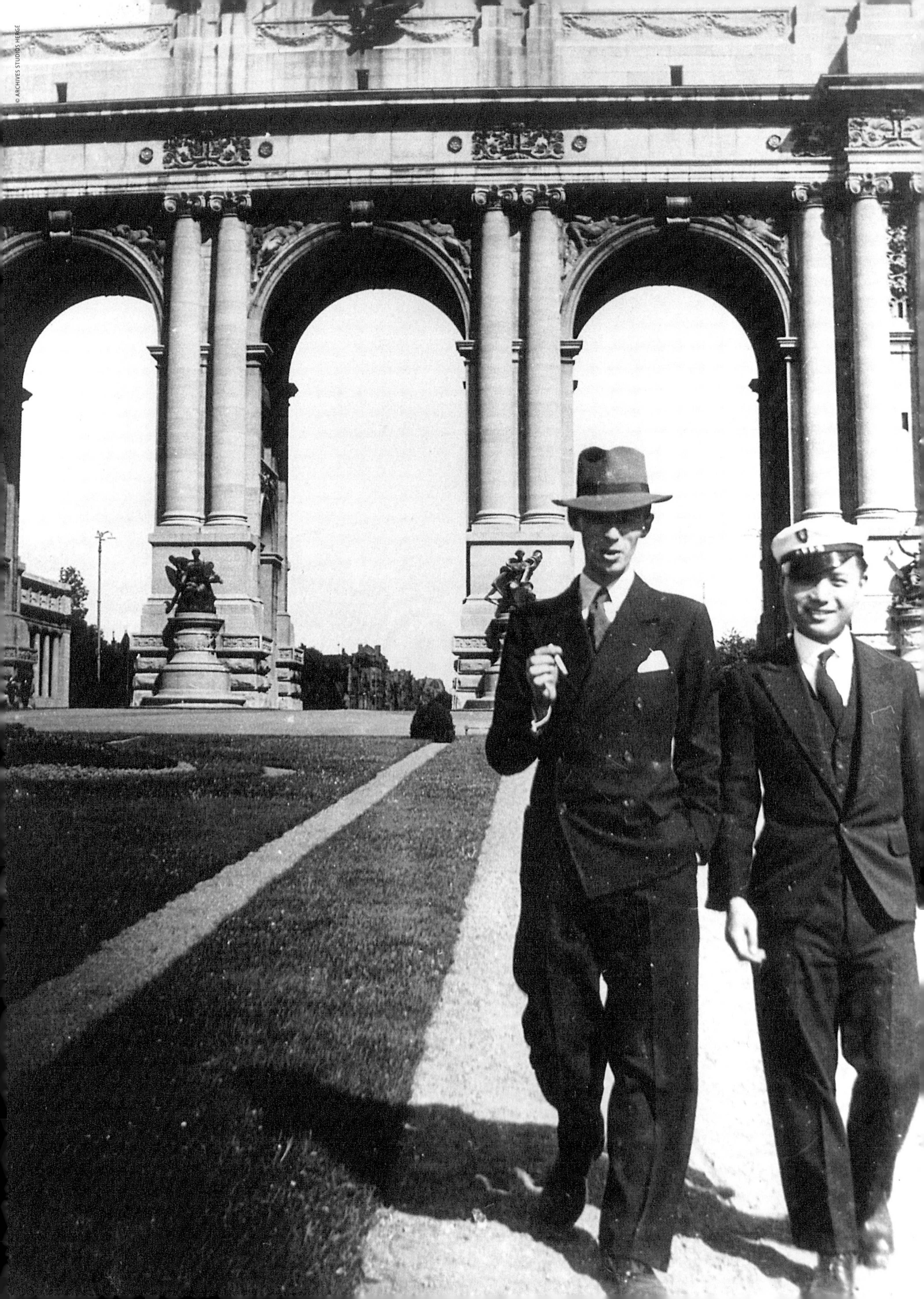

CHAPTER SIX

Oriental attraction

If there was to be one meeting that more than any other affected Hergé's work, as well as his view of life, it occurred on Tuesday, 1 May 1934, at five o'clock in the afternoon. In a development that could have come straight out of a Tintin adventure, where a mysterious stranger rings the doorbell of the reporter's flat at 26 Labrador Road, a young Chinese rang the buzzer of Hergé's apartment in the Rue Knapen. His name was Chang Chong-chen, and he was a promising twenty-six-year-old sculpture student at the Brussels Académie des Beaux-Arts. Over cups of tea – China, one presumes – the two similarly aged young men discussed the priests who had put them in touch and then Tintin's forthcoming trip to China, for which Hergé hoped for Chang's help. Between the Jesuit-educated Chinese art student and the intellectually curious Belgian there was a remarkable meeting of minds, and an instant and special friendship. This was unusual in the case of Hergé, who, by nature reserved and reticent, normally needed time to establish a friendship to which subsequently he would remain fiercely loyal.

A MISGUIDED VIEW

Hergé had twice before depicted Chinamen in *The Adventures of Tintin*, and on each occasion had fallen for the clichéd Western view of the cruel, pigtailed and slant-eyed Oriental. In *Tintin in the Land of the Soviets*, the Bolsheviks employ Chinese torturers, refined in the methods of exacting excruciating pain. 'Mister Tintin, you are going to be tortured, to help you reveal the purpose of your journey!' the communist prison governor tells Tintin, who is led down to a torture chamber replete with every conceivable device to inflict horrifying pain. The room, with its obligatory rack, red-hot pokers, pincers and whips, is overseen by two glum Chinese, dressed *à la Chinoise* and with long pigtails trailing from their otherwise shaven craniums. Most sinisterly a disembodied head even lurks in the corner of Hergé's picture. Despite their evil appearance, however, the oriental torturers are no match for Snowy and Tintin, who soon turn the tables on them, prompting expletives and howls in mock Chinese – Hergé's attempt at imitating Chinese characters.

There is a similar unfortunate episode in *Tintin in America*, when the Chicago gangsters hand over the reporter – kidnapped at the banquet held in his honour – and Snowy to another pair of Chinese executioners, this time charged with sending Tintin to the bottom of Lake Michigan weighed down with a pair of dumb-bells. 'As for your dirty cur, I will leave him to him my yellow friends: they are very partial to little dogs,' declares the gangster boss chillingly. Poor Snowy has a vision of himself appearing on a plate surrounded by deep-fried vegetables before the two salivating Chinamen. They then drop the bound and weighted Tintin into the water. In the later, 1945, colour edition of the adventure, the Chinese were edited out, with an all-American thug substituted in their place. It is interesting, though, that in these first works, when a torturer or executioner was required, Hergé immediately recruited Chinese, who to him clearly had an international reputation for brutality even far from their homeland, whether in Russia or America.

Two glum Chinese dressed
à la Chinoise and with long pigtails
trailing from their shaven craniums.

LEFT
Hergé and Chang in Brussels, 1934.

On his return from America, Tintin is 'interviewed' in *Le Petit Vingtième* about his future travel plans and declares that he will be 'setting out shortly for China'. He jokes with his interviewer, who talks of Chinese torturers and Snowy's possible abduction, not just by gangsters but by gourmets, as 'apparently in that country they eat dogs as well as birds' nests'. Tintin reassures him that Snowy, like his master, knows how to defend himself.

Among the drawings accompanying the article published in the weekly on 24 November 1932 is one showing a skull-faced Chinaman brandishing a sword and chasing a terrified Snowy. He is indistinguishable from one of the executioners encountered in the original version of *Tintin in America*.

Such extreme, racist parodies of the Chinese were typical at the time in Europe, where knowledge of the 'Middle Kingdom' was minimal and limited to the worst excesses of the Boxer Rising. They were nevertheless beneath Hergé and his natural striving towards objectivity and accuracy. Thanks to Chang these errors were to be put right.

AN END TO MISCONCEPTIONS

After Tintin pulls the half-drowned boy Chang out of the floodwaters of the Yangtze-Kiang, they talk about each other's misconceptions. 'Different peoples don't know enough about each other,' Tintin tells Chang, echoing no doubt the conversation Hergé would have had with the real Chang. 'Lots of Europeans still believe that all Chinese are cunning and cruel and wear pig-tails, are always inventing tortures, and eating rotten eggs and swallows' nests…' It was a view Hergé himself was propagating only a couple of years earlier.

The boy Chang is surprised that a white person has saved his life. 'I thought all white devils were wicked, like those who killed my grandfather and grandmother long ago. During the War of Righteous and Harmonious Fists, my father said.'

'The Boxer Rebellion, yes,' Tintin interjects. The Boxer Rising derived its name from the bands of fanatical Chinese nationalists – known as Boxers – who in 1900 at the instigation of the Empress Dowager besieged the foreign legations in Peking, and murdered European missionaries and thousands of Chinese converts. An international punitive force was dispatched to quell the rebellion and Peking was captured on 14 August 1900, after which China agreed to pay a large indemnity. In the West, China had not had a good press since, something Japan, with ambitions in Manchuria and beyond, was able to take advantage of but which Hergé would expose with the help of Chang in *The Blue Lotus*.

BELOW LEFT
After Tintin pulls the half-drowned boy Chang out of the floodwaters of the Yangtze-Kiang, they talk about each other's misconceptions.

BELOW RIGHT
The boy Chang is surprised that a white person has saved his life.

CHAPTER SIX **ORIENTAL ATTRACTION**

Despite the setback of the uprising, Christian missionaries remained active in China.
The Jesuits were in the forefront, and it was a Jesuit education which the real Chang received in Shanghai.
The Christian College of Xujiahui where the young Chang went to school (right).

Tintin is interviewed about his future travel plans.

Despite the setback of the uprising, Christian missionaries remained active in China. The Jesuits were in the forefront, and it was a Jesuit education which the real Chang received in Shanghai. There were regular contacts between Belgian priests and Chinese Catholics, some of whom travelled to Europe and Belgium for their studies. It was one such priest, Father Léon Gosset, chaplain to the Chinese students at the University of Louvain, who was behind the introduction to Chang. Together with his students, he was an avid follower of Tintin's adventures and, learning from *Le Petit Vingtième* that the reporter's next destination was to be China, was anxious that Hergé should not disappoint them with clichés and inaccuracies. He had already transgressed – as far as portraying the Chinese was concerned – in two of the first three Tintin books. Gosset wrote to Hergé, expressing his concern, and suggesting that he could meet some of his students so as to gain a better-informed picture of their country. Hergé, with his journalistic desire for accuracy, was ripe for such a suggestion, which dovetailed well with the research he had already begun for Tintin's next adventure.

While Hergé allowed himself and Tintin a break after *Cigars of the Pharaoh*, the recently concluded adventure, on 8 March 1934 *Le Petit Vingtième* published a short question-and-answer sequence in response to the impatient concern of readers at the reporter's absence, enjoying a 'well-earned' rest in India as a guest of the Maharaja of Gaipajama at his magnificent palace. It began by asking: 'What are your plans, Tintin? Are you going to marry some oriental princess and remain in that magnificent country, living the life of a pasha, lounging all day long on cushions, surrounded by servants fanning away the flies?'

Tintin assures readers that such a life is not for him and that soon he would be setting out again to pick up the trail of the opium traffickers that seemed to lead to the Far East, prompting the question: 'Aren't you afraid of the Chinese, Tintin?'

To which Hergé, having just received Father Gosset's letter, replies carefully: 'Scared of the Chinese? Obviously there are all sorts, as with Europeans, but the Chinese in general are charming people, very polite, highly cultured and most hospitable. Many of the missionaries I have encountered on my travels have spoken of a China they love greatly. And it is an error to believe that all Chinese are false, cruel, etc.'

A FRESH APPROACH

Hergé had got the message and was on the road to reform that was consolidated and continued when he went to Louvain and met Father Gosset and two of his students, 'Arnold' Chiao Cheng-chi, an expert on Chinese theatre, and his fiancée 'Suzanne' Lin. Gosset also recommended a meeting with the art student Chang Chong-chen, to whom Hergé wrote on 30 March. In due course Chang replied and the May Day rendezvous was settled on.

Another priest with whom Hergé had long enjoyed a rapport was to play a key role in his new desire to portray the Chinese conscientiously. Hergé had first met Father Édouard Neut of the Abbey of St André at Loppem near Bruges on a school retreat in 1923, and had returned there in 1931 to consider his engagement to Germaine. Neut was knowledgeable about China and was close to an interesting and learned character, Father Pierre Célestin Lou, previously Lou Tseng-tsiang, a former Chinese diplomat and government minister, who had become a monk at St André after the death of his Belgian wife. Hergé and Neut now exchanged letters about the plan to send Tintin to China, and the priest was delighted by the author's good intentions, which he believed offered the prospect of 'a work of inter-racial understanding' and 'real friendship between yellow and white people'. He sent Hergé books and a newspaper article to further his understanding. One of the volumes was *Aux Origines du conflit mandchou* (The Origins of the Manchurian Conflict) by another priest, Father Thadée, which explained the background to the Japanese aggression in Manchuria.

FIRST REVELATIONS

Two years earlier, following a report in *Le Petit Vingtième* about the Japanese invasion of China and occupation of Shanghai, a reader had suggested sending Tintin there. The newspaper's response then was that it was out of the question as it was much too dangerous. Now, however, Hergé felt the time was right to draw attention to Japanese warmongering and the plight of the Chinese.

Though for the most part Europeans remained ill informed about developments in China and life there, a number of books by European writers had been published in the last few years on this distant and mysterious land. Some, such as *La Condition humaine* (The Human Condition) by André Malraux, with its picture of life in Shanghai, Hergé cannot have failed to

ABOVE
Albert Londres, the celebrated foreign correspondent on whom Tintin was to some extent modelled, sent numerous dispatches back from China.

CHAPTER SIX **ORIENTAL ATTRACTION**

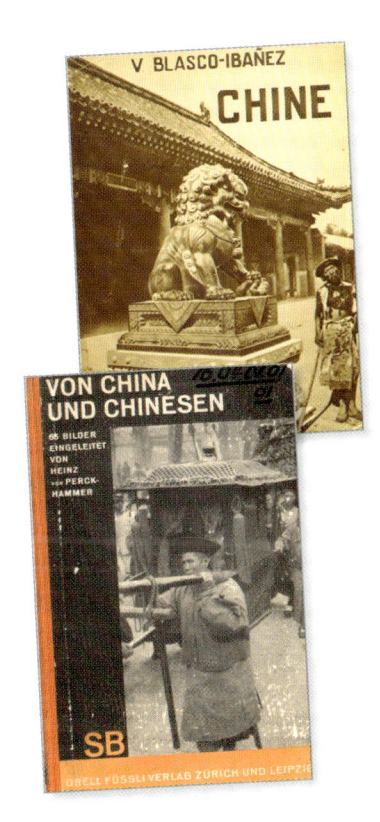

notice, for it was the winner of the prestigious Prix Goncourt literary prize in 1933. Malraux himself became a great Tintin enthusiast, and after the Second World War, as culture minister under President Charles de Gaulle, reported the general as saying that he considered Tintin to be his 'only international rival'.

Even if it appeared only sporadically, there was more from China in the newspapers than in the past. Albert Londres, the celebrated foreign correspondent on whom Tintin was to some extent modelled, sent numerous dispatches back, though not his final report from Manchuria and Shanghai, which, he told friends enigmatically, was on 'a subject more explosive than dynamite'. He boarded the newly built liner *Georges-Philippar* at the end of March 1932 in Shanghai to bring his story back in person, but he never reached home. After a mysterious fire on board, the *Georges-Philippar* sank off Aden in the middle of May with the loss of many lives, including Londres, whose body was never recovered and whose secrets went with him to a watery grave. It was a tale as mysterious as any faced by Tintin.

The cinema too provided inspiration, with a flurry of Chinese-themed films, including Josef von Sternberg's *Shanghai Express* of 1932, starring Marlene Dietrich, from which the title that Hergé eventually settled on for his new adventure would seem to have come. The rebel leader who is holding Dietrich hostage receives an enigmatic telegram: 'Blue Lotus lost must have red blossoms midnight.' As a flower, a blue lotus is unknown. The striking cover for *The Blue Lotus*, originally with a red dragon on a black background (the colours are reversed in the later colour edition), was also connected with von Sternberg's film, for a remarkably similar version featured as a backdrop to a picture of Anna May Wong, Dietrich's co-star, on the cover of the illustrated weekly *A-Z*, which caught Hergé's eye.

Expanding his reading list on China, Hergé picked up copies of Blasco Ibañez's *Chine* (China), published by Flammarion, and the copiously illustrated *Von China und Chinesen* (On China and the Chinese) by the German Heinz von Perkhammer. Of greater value than any reference books, however, were the meetings with Chang, which resumed on 13 May and then became institutionalised as a regular Sunday afternoon fixture, with Germaine preparing tea and pancakes, which the Chinese art student was particularly partial to.

ABOVE LEFT
Expanding his reading list on China.

ABOVE RIGHT
Of greater value than any reference books were the meetings with Chang. Here on 13 May 1934.

THE ADVENTURES OF HERGÉ, CREATOR OF TINTIN

ABOVE
As a student Chang was highly regarded by his professors and popular with his peers. Arriving in Brussels in October 1931, he enrolled and passed the exams for the Académie des Beaux-Arts.

RIGHT
He would bring gifts of Chinese drawing manuals and paintbrushes, and would explain techniques.

DISCOVERING THE EAST

Chang did not want any remuneration for his visits; it was a pleasure and a duty for him to explain to Hergé all he could about his country and culture. He would bring gifts of Chinese drawing manuals and paintbrushes, and would explain techniques. They would talk about history and geography, art and poetry. Hergé found himself falling under the spell of a philosophy that he found more attractive than anything the West had to offer.

He acknowledged his debt to Chang many years later after finally tracing him again following an interval of some forty years during which they had lost contact. In a letter dated 1 May 1975, Hergé wrote of his gratitude 'not only for the help you gave me at the time with my work, but also and above all for everything that without realising you brought me. Thanks to you, my life took a new orientation. You made me discover a whole range of things, poetry, the feeling of man's unity with the universe'.

There was something very special and touching about the Westernised Chinese student – a French-speaker and devout Catholic – introducing a Belgian of the same age from a very conventional, bourgeois background to the wisdom of the East. To the end of his life, Hergé retained a deep and dominant interest in Taoism and Zen Buddhism.

Apart from their similar ages, they had much in common. They were open minded, they had a strong sense of humour and they both dressed smartly. The snapshots of them together during their burgeoning friendship in 1934 demonstrate the importance they attached to appearance. Hergé, the son of a boys' outfitter, is invariably well suited and turned out, and Chang is impeccable with either a bow tie or a carefully knotted regular one, and, adding a dapper touch, his favourite cream-coloured yachting cum student cap. He would even keep a tie on during painting and sculpture classes, something that was remarked on by his fellow students.

As a student Chang was highly regarded by his professors and popular with his peers. Arriving in Brussels in October 1931, he enrolled and passed the exams (into the top painting class) for the Académie des Beaux-Arts. Subsequently he entered the sculpture class of Professor Égide Rombeaux, an imposing and encouraging teacher who had been impressed by the feeling for matter and volume Chang showed in his painting. In 1933 he won the painting prize for the second year running, as well as gaining an award from the Chinese embassy in Belgium for his painting, *The Eve of the Retreat*. Ironically this painting was among the works of his destroyed in 1966 during the so-called Cultural Revolution. In January 1934 he won the Académie's first prize for sculpture, and the following month he was elected secretary and spokesman of the Association of Chinese Students in Belgium. He was certainly making the most of his time studying in Belgium.

Additionally he was absorbing all the art he could in the Brussels museums, on trips to other Belgian cities and during a four-week stay in Paris. He was mightily impressed by the great paintings of Rubens and moved by the work of Van Eyck. In the French capital he was bowled over by the bronze and marble sculptures of Rodin, which were to influence his own work.

HOMESICKNESS

He was, however, also desperately homesick. He wrote home frequently and sent back examples of his work – drawings, paintings and smaller pieces of sculpture – but he was pained by the news of the Japanese invasion, which came as he was travelling to Europe. In fact, the date on which he embarked for Europe, 18 September 1931, was the very day Japanese agents sabotaged the railway line, the famous 'Moukden incident' that gave Japan its pretext for invading Manchuria. In *The Blue Lotus* the sabotage is witnessed by Tintin.

The snapshots of them together demonstrate the importance they attached to appearance.

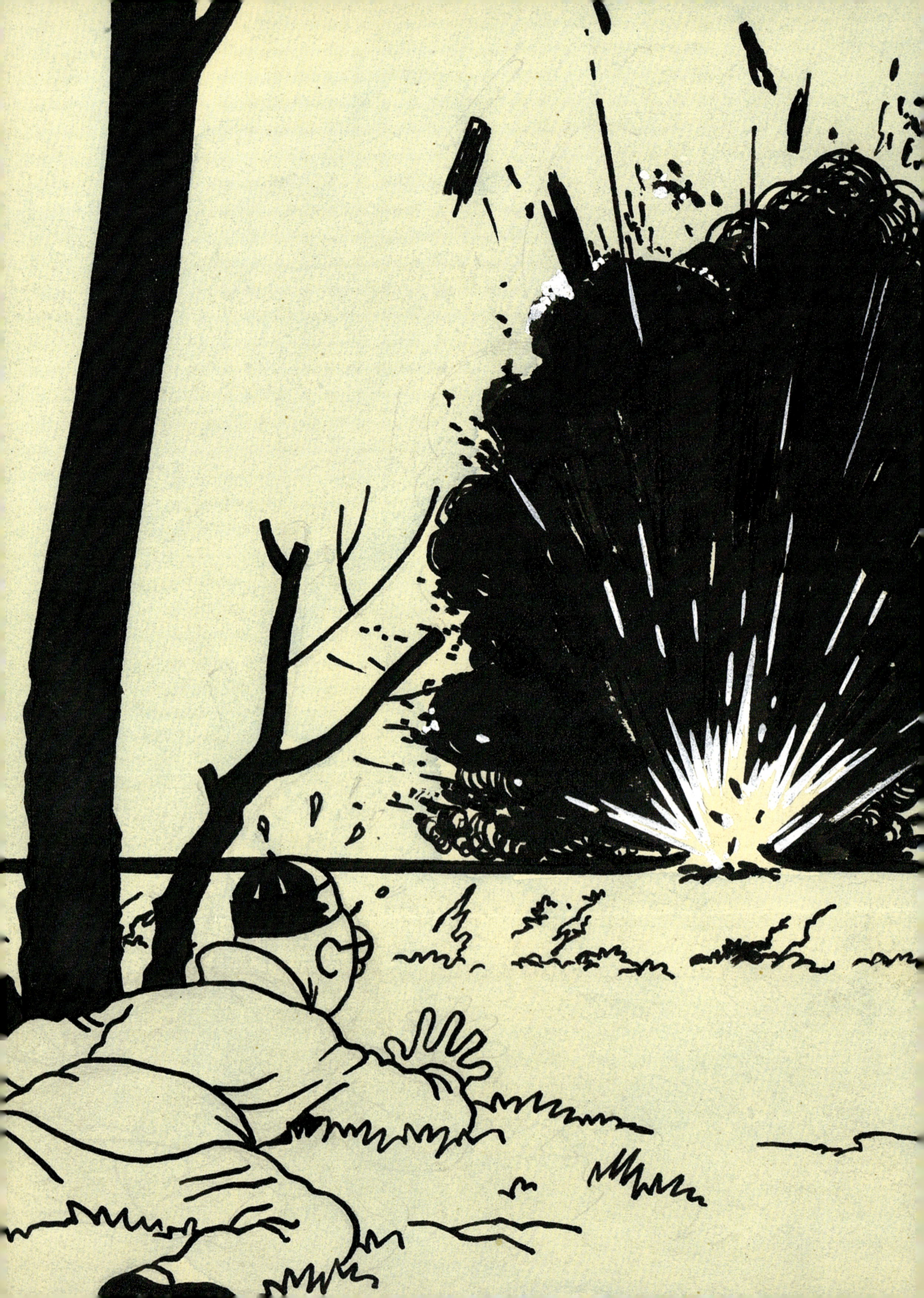

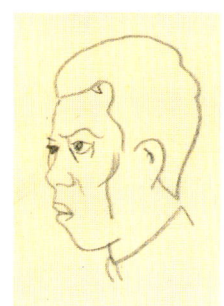

CHAPTER SIX **ORIENTAL ATTRACTION**

Hergé began sketching facial types – distinguishing between Chinese and Japanese.

Chang gained some solace from his contacts with the sinophile clergy, with Father Gosset, Father Neut and above all Father Pierre Célestin Lou (Lou Tseng-tsieng), who was a friend of his great-uncle Ma Xiangbo. He would visit the Abbey of St André at Loppem near Bruges, and was there for the ordination of Father Célestin in June 1933, presenting him with a sculpture he had made of St Francis Xavier, the Spanish Jesuit missionary who set out to bring Christianity to China in the sixteenth century. The sculpture shows the saint holding a cross up to China, as he is said to have done just before he died in 1552.

Now, added to all his other activities, Chang agreed to help Hergé send Tintin to Shanghai. It was to be a bigger, more carefully prepared undertaking than any Hergé and Tintin had undertaken before, made possible by Chang's intervention. Having gathered his documentary material, with Chang's guidance Hergé began sketching facial types – distinguishing between Chinese and Japanese – and typical street or market scenes. More preliminary sketches exist for this Tintin adventure than for any other, and while most are certainly by Hergé, some – and he could not later always distinguish which – are by his new Chinese friend. Apart from ensuring that Hergé captured the mood and was always accurate, Chang proved himself invaluable in providing the Chinese writing and ideograms that are skilfully woven into the scenes. No longer are the characters and lettering poor, meaningless imitations drawn *à la Chinoise*, as in *Tintin in the Land of the Soviets*: they are authentic, legible to the Chinese reader and with often pertinent and pregnant meaning.

97

Chang would take away from his Sunday afternoon visits scenes already discussed and prepared by Hergé in which he would insert graffiti, posters and advertisements, banners, shop signs, domestic proverbs and street signs, as well as occasional Chinese dialogue.

CHINESE SUBTEXT

Chang would take away from his Sunday afternoon visits scenes already discussed and prepared by Hergé, in which he would insert Chinese writing, to be returned the following week. He would fill in graffiti, posters and advertisements, banners, shop signs, domestic proverbs and street signs, as well as occasional Chinese dialogue. Chang had been taught the art of calligraphy before he left for Europe by his great-uncle Ma Xiangbo, who lived to a great age, dying in his one hundredth year in 1939, the year Chang completed a bust of his venerable mentor.

Tintin asks a Shanghai policeman for directions and receives a reply in Chinese: 'It's the second road down there.' The rickshaw runner about to hurtle accidentally into the odious Gibbons exclaims: 'Excuse me, Sir!' as a wall poster behind declares, 'Abolish the unequal treaties!'

Another poster, behind the bully Gibbons when an indignant Tintin breaks his walking cane in two, exhorts: 'Down with imperialism!' As the car races off after the failed attempt to gun down Tintin, another sign attached to a telegraph post urges: 'Boycott Japanese Goods!' Later, a prisoner of the Japanese, Tintin is paraded through the streets bearing a block clamped around his neck with the inscription: 'Condemned to death for opposing the Japanese army'. The street scenes are peppered with allusions and slogans that Chang, mindful of the Japanese occupation of his home city, must have relished as his contribution to resistance.

Some of the most delightful inscriptions are the simplest, evoking local colour perfectly – a lightbulb poster bearing the words 'Electricity Siemens' and Tintin giving an address to a rickshaw operator in front of a shop sign declaring 'Clocks and watches repaired'. Later Tintin stops for refreshment at a simple establishment under the sign: 'Here one can drink and eat small portions'. Chinese wisdom is apparent too in posters with such proverbs as 'If you are ill, you will not be able to achieve your goals' or 'To own a thousand acres of land is worth less than a decent job'.

Not surprisingly, the Shanghai portrayed by Hergé, and verified by Chang, is readily recognisable from photographs of the 1930s, some of which he used as documentation. There is even an Odeon cinema with a Western classical pediment near the city gates (page 40), a conspicuous landmark repeated at the end of 1945 in the first frame of a strip cartoon detective thriller – 'One night in Shanghai…' – begun by Hergé with Edgar-Pierre Jacobs, but subsequently discontinued.

This was a new approach to Tintin; there was nothing haphazard or left to chance as in the previous adventures, where Hergé admitted that he did not always know where the story was heading, or which twist or turn it would take next. He had previously been working from one week to the next to satisfy his tight deadlines. The result was certainly spontaneous and exciting, but without the depth that he was now able to bring with increased preparation. *The Blue Lotus*, with its new working methods, was a catalyst marking a switch to increased realism. Hergé himself acknowledged that it marked the beginning of his 'documentalist' period. Proof of its more considered quality came when it was put into book form, initially in black and white and then after the war in colour, when, unlike with the earlier adventures, no significant cuts, adaptations or changes were necessary. It was a perfectly constructed work, which raised the strip cartoon, of which Hergé was the great pioneer in Europe, to a new level.

The drawing was more disciplined as a result of the many preliminary sketches, the setting was more exact and the story had a political background that reflected current affairs and gave it topicality. There was too, thanks to Chang, a marriage of artistic styles: Hergé's own natural talent with the awareness in Chinese art of giving life to objects through line. It was in *The Blue Lotus* that Hergé developed the practice and advocacy of *la ligne claire* – the clear line – that became the hallmark of his work and made it so influential to other artists.

ABOVE
Chang had been taught the art of calligraphy before he left for Europe by his great-uncle Ma Xiangbo.

RIGHT
'Condemned to death for opposing the Japanese army.'

LEFT
'One night in Shanghai…' begun by Hergé with Edgar-Pierre Jacobs.

THE ADVENTURES OF HERGÉ, CREATOR OF TINTIN

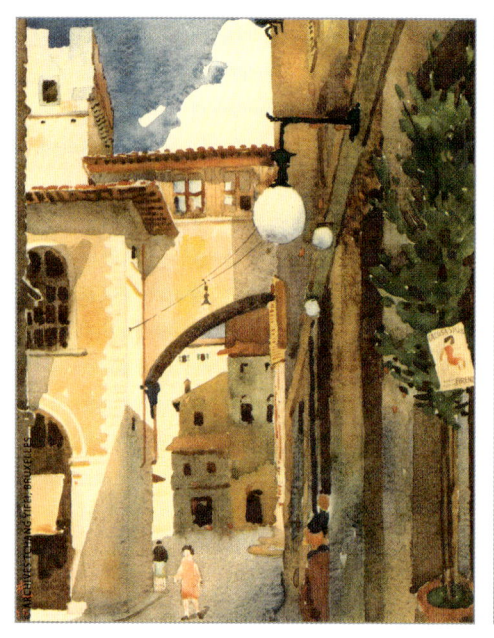

Before returning home Chang undertook a trip around Europe. He took his sketchbook and watercolours with him and produced limpid impressions of the sun-dappled sights seen through Chinese eyes.

Back in Shanghai with great-uncle Ma Xiangbo (centre) and artist friends and writers.

ANTICIPATING EVENTS

Hergé's increased absorption in the subject he was tackling brought understanding and with it an extraordinary prophetic quality that he was to demonstrate on a number of occasions: in *The Blue Lotus* (1934), where his portrayal of the build-up of Japanese military and imperial ambitions anticipates the attack on Pearl Harbor seven years later; in *King Ottokar's Sceptre* (1938), where his account of a planned fascist takeover and invasion plotted by a certain Müsstler (amalgamation of Mussolini and Hitler) came months before Hitler's well stage-managed takeover of Czechoslovakia and invasion of Poland; and *Explorers on the Moon* (1953), where Tintin steps on to the Moon in circumstances remarkably similar to Neil Armstrong's – and equally hazardous – sixteen years later. This was possible because Hergé, like a good journalist, had such an understanding of his subject that he could project it forward. This gave the Tintin adventures an extraordinary, and perhaps unexpected, credibility.

Hergé's intense, fruitful partnership with Chang was, however, to be of limited duration – just over a year – for, completing his studies, the Chinese artist was anxious to go back to face the political turmoil at home, and to be with his family again, particularly his influential nonagenarian great-uncle. By the summer of 1935 he was packing up his bags – he shipped thirteen trunks full of belongings and examples of his artwork to Shanghai – and was preparing for the return voyage home after an absence of almost four years. Having arrived via Marseilles and a rather disagreeable train trip across France, sharing a compartment with rowdy French conscripts, he decided to set out this time, like Marco Polo, from Venice. First, though, he would undertake an educationally necessary trip around Europe, to Holland, England, France, Germany and Austria, visiting the major art museums, culminating in the obligatory – for an artist – Grand Tour of Italy, seeing as many of its historic cities and principal museums as possible. He took his sketchbook and watercolours with him and produced limpid impressions of the sun-dappled sights seen through Chinese eyes.

Chang left Brussels in July from the Gare du Nord, the station where Tintin was fêted on his returns from Russia and the Congo. Having modestly and gratefully declined the offer of co-authorship with him, he would leave Hergé on his own to complete *The Blue Lotus* that October. It included the final episode where, just in time, Chang comes to the rescue of Tintin, who is about to be beheaded, shooting the sword from the executioner's hand. As the train pulled out from the station, he saw a familiar figure running down the platform, waving his hat and shouting words he could not hear – it was Hergé. It was a poignant, almost cinematic farewell, for though the two friends would write to each other – Chang sent cards from Italy with his impressions and Hergé wrote to him in Shanghai – world events overwhelmed them both, and as war broke out in both East and West they lost contact completely. Had it not been for war – and his considerable workload – Hergé might have been able to visit Chang in Shanghai, for none other than Song Meilin, the wife of the Nationalist generalissimo Chiang Kai-shek, was so impressed by *The Blue Lotus* and its championing of the Chinese cause that she invited Hergé to visit as an official guest. Finally, in 1973, he was able to take up the offer, though with the Chinese mainland long under communist rule the invitation was now limited to Nationalist Taiwan. Ironically, this visit subsequently created complications and ultimately prevented him going to Shanghai when, a couple of years later, he found out – after an interval of forty years – that Chang was indeed alive and well and living in his home city.

Tintin steps on to the Moon in circumstances remarkably similar to Neil Armstrong's sixteen years later.

LEFT
By the summer of 1935 Chang was packing up his bags. He left Brussels in July from the Gare du Nord, the station where Tintin was fêted on his returns from Russia and the Congo.

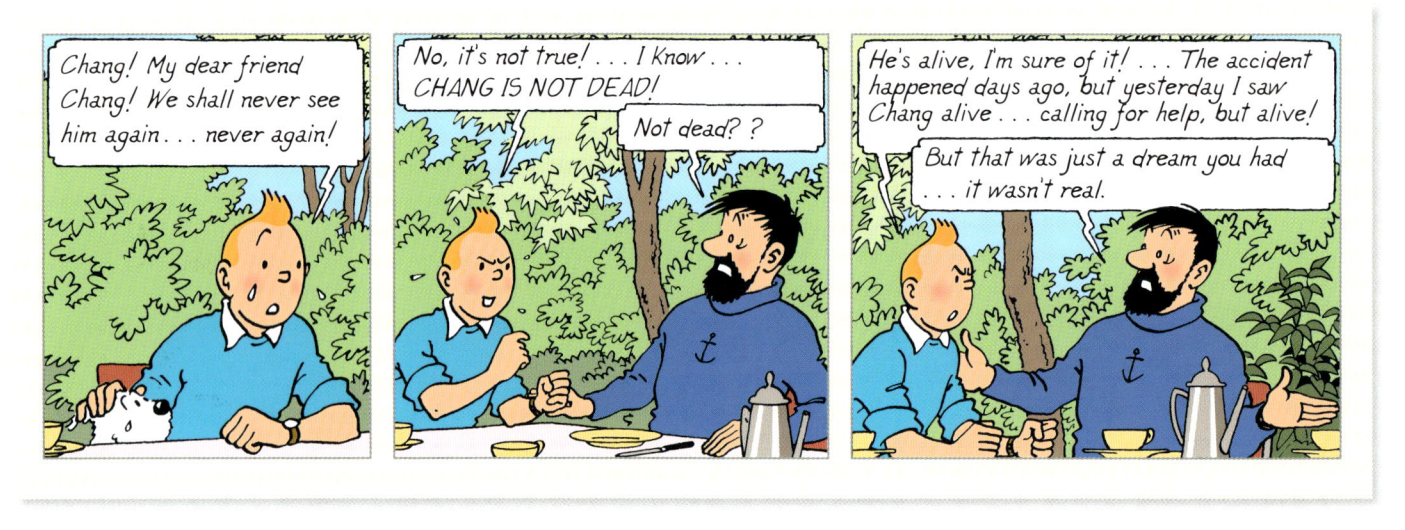

> Tintin never wavers in his determination to find Chang, who he feels certain is still alive.

AN INTENSE FRIENDSHIP

The friendship between Hergé and Chang was short, intense and largely intellectual. There was no intimacy. Hergé, as ever reserved, would always *vouvoyer* his Chinese friend, using the less personal form of address in French – *vous* as opposed to *tu* – a formality that no doubt was more natural to Chang too. Yet there was a deeper significance to the friendship than to any other Hergé struck up, for Chang had opened up a whole new world to him. As the years passed and Hergé, with his share of tribulation, had reason to consider the nature of friendship, he often thought of Chang. Attempts to re-establish contact failed. If in life he could not find his long-lost friend, however, he would rediscover him in literature, in a new Tintin adventure.

By the mid 1950s, hovering on the brink of total nervous collapse and finding it almost impossible to continue work, Hergé sought help from a Dr Franz Ricklin, a pupil of Carl Gustav Jung, whom he admired greatly. His long marriage to Germaine had reached breaking point, yet his Catholic Boy Scout upbringing taught him to value loyalty above all. He had had several brief, unsatisfactory relationships with younger women that left him feeling profoundly guilty. The doctor advised complete rest and a halt to Tintin.

Hergé was to ignore doctor's orders, however, and persist with Tintin. This time he would take him to the snow-covered Himalayas to find and save his never forgotten friend Chang, whom he had pulled from the floodwaters of the Yangtze-Kiang, for a second time. The result, *Tintin in Tibet*, was the most personally significant Tintin adventure since *The Blue Lotus*. It immediately became, not surprisingly, his favourite.

Among the symptoms of his depression were nightmares, in which everything would be overpoweringly white, so called 'white-outs', from which he would wake terrified in a cold sweat. Hergé often had dreams and sometimes noted their contents, but these were unbearable. In a serendipitous therapy he eliminated the haunting whiteness from his subconscious by depicting in the new adventure the great white expanses of the Himalayas that Tintin traverses in his rock-solid but apparently vain hope of finding Chang, presumed to have perished in an airliner crash. That and a blossoming romance with Fanny Vlamynck, one of the colourists recently taken on at the studios, were enough to put him on the road to recovery.

RIGHT
In a serendipitous therapy Hergé eliminated the haunting whiteness from his subconscious by depicting in the new adventure the great white expanses of the Himalayas.

CHAPTER SIX **ORIENTAL ATTRACTION**

CATHARSIS

So for a second time Chang became associated with a fundamental change – for the better – in Hergé's life, even if on this occasion it was only Chang the character, the friend of Tintin. *Tintin in Tibet* is a remarkable story, 'a hymn to friendship' in Hergé's own words, where the author was able to explore some of the greater issues in life and pursue his own fascination with telepathy, dreams, visions and levitation. Tintin never wavers in his determination to find Chang, who he feels certain is still alive. He shouts out his name, on seeing him in a nightmare, after which 'Chang' recurs on twenty-eight other occasions in a variety of forms over the next six pages. It is as if there is telepathic contact between Chang in distress and his friend. Then Captain Haddock, who, roped to Tintin on a sheer rock face, has lost his foothold, is prepared to cut the rope and make the ultimate self-sacrifice to enable the reporter to survive. This is a Tintin adventure with a difference. There are neither villains nor violence, only huge challenges to overcome and proof of unshakeable friendship to be given. There are fewer characters – the Thom(p)sons are absent for the first time since *Cigars of the Pharaoh* and Professor Calculus only has a walk-on role – but Chang returns for the first time since Tintin waved a tearful farewell to him on the Shanghai quayside, and a warm-hearted but misunderstood creature, the Yeti, is introduced. No doubt Tintin was, as in other cases, anticipating real life in finding the fabled Abominable Snowman before anyone else.

Chang survived all the upheavals of war, communism and the Cultural Revolution.

The army is omnipresent in communist China during the 1960s.

Young people interpreting revolutionary songs, intended to educate the masses.

CHAPTER SIX **ORIENTAL ATTRACTION**

BELOW
Chang was still living at the same address he had returned to in 1935.

Hergé's introduction to oriental poetry, literature and philosophy by Chang in 1934 was a revelation from which he never looked back. A deep interest in Taoism and Zen Buddhism – later shared with Fanny – followed and now, as he plunged himself into books about Tibet, his enthusiasm was rekindled. As usual his research was thorough, whether on the Tibetan monasteries or accounts of the Yeti. He supplemented this by seeking out and collecting oriental art, including exquisite Chinese vases, articles in jade and the Tibetan Buddha that was to find its place on his bookshelves. His own dream experiences led to his absorption in the phenomena of dreams and visions. He was fascinated by examples of levitation. When the monk Blessed Lightning levitates and has a vision, it is only because Hergé had carefully studied reports of such happenings at Tibetan monasteries. It is as accurate as his depiction of the monastic musical instruments and dress. Furthermore his focus on Tibet once again reflected world events. The Tintin adventure began in September 1958, as communist China's effective annexation of the Himalayan state led to civil disturbances and the dramatic escape of Tibet's political and spiritual leader, the Dalai Lama, to exile in India in March 1959.

DREAMS AND NIGHTMARES

Dreams were of particular interest to Hergé and *Tintin in Tibet* was not the first adventure to feature them. Already in *Cigars of the Pharaoh* there is a memorable sequence when Tintin falls into a narcotics-induced coma. In *The Crab with the Golden Claws*, Tintin has a terrifying dream of a sun-crazed Captain Haddock trying to uncork him with a corkscrew, while manipulated nightmares explain the mystery of *The Seven Crystal Balls*, revealed in its sequel, *Prisoners of the Sun*. Then there is Madame Yamilah's vision of the photographer's fate in *The Seven Crystal Balls*. Tintin, moreover, has an extraordinary nightmare sequence over the first three frames of page 23 of *Prisoners of the Sun*, when he sleeps by the old Inca tomb. Later Captain Haddock, sometimes the alter ego of Hergé himself, dreams of a parrot or bird-like incarnation of Bianca Castafiore in both *The Castafiore Emerald* and the final, unfinished *Tintin and Alph-Art*. Dreams and hypnotism, though this time transmitted by alien forces, feature less convincingly in *Flight 714*, where Hergé indulged in exploring the possibility of extraterrestrial influences.

It all demonstrated his open-mindedness and willingness to explore the unconventional and unusual, something that was first brought out by those meetings with Chang in 1934–5. Now with *Tintin in Tibet* he was reliving that old friendship in fiction. Chang's name is found carved in the rock in the Yeti's cave. Hergé was, however, none the wiser about the existence of the real Chang. When he went to Chinese restaurants in Brussels or Paris he would optimistically take old photographs of Chang and the drawing of his name as it appeared on the rock inscription, hoping to find someone who might have some information about him. It was a hopeless task, it seemed.

Then, out of the blue, early in 1975 at a dinner party in Brussels, Hergé found himself sitting by Pierre Wei, a French-speaking Chinese. He asked him his stock question, whether he knew a sculptor called Chang Chong-chen who lived in Shanghai before the war. Wei paused to think, repeated the name and then came out with the extraordinary revelation that Chang Chong-chen had been his best man in Shanghai more than twenty years earlier. He too had lost touch with him but would ask his brother, who lived in Shanghai, to find out more. The brother visited Chang, reported him safe and well and still living at the same address he had returned to in 1935! Hergé had finally rediscovered Chang, who had survived all the upheavals of war, communism and the Cultural Revolution, which had seen him degraded and much of his work destroyed.

REDISCOVERY

On 1 May 1975 – it had been on May Day 1934 that Chang had first rung his doorbell – Hergé sat down and wrote that long, deeply felt letter to his old friend, acknowledging and listing his debt to him, and telling how in the intervening years he had persevered in his pursuit of Chinese philosophy and art, which continued to be of great significance to him. He added that he had very recently decided to take Chinese lessons. He related how he had been thinking of him and how Tintin had searched for and found his friend Chang in the Himalayas fifteen years earlier. Under separate cover, he sent him copies of *Tintin in Tibet* and *The Blue Lotus*, which had been completed and appeared in book form – and subsequently in colour – only after Chang's return to Shanghai. While the letter reached Chang, the books did not for some time. The first package disappeared completely; the second was returned as a prohibited import and only after representations at the Chinese embassy in Brussels did a third pair of books get through, still subject to a great deal of bureaucracy.

In his letter Hergé detailed the debt he felt he owed Chang. 'Thanks to you, finally, I discovered – after Marco Polo! – China, its civilisation, its thinking, its art and artists. At this very moment I am immersed in Tao Tö-king and Chouang Tseu, and I owe it to you!'

The correspondence between the two friends continued, but ultimately Hergé's hopes of visiting Shanghai, the city he had depicted so conscientiously in 1934, foundered on the fact that he had travelled to Nationalist Taiwan in 1973, something unacceptable to the communist Chinese, and then, as time passed, on his declining health. If there was to be a reunion between Hergé and Chang, it would have to be organised differently. A leading Belgian television journalist, Gérard Valet, undertook to lobby the Chinese authorities and to bring Chang to Brussels. His efforts were finally rewarded when Chang, accompanied by his son Xueren, arrived at Brussels' Zaventem airport on 18 March 1981. Appropriately, there was a media melee worthy of a Tintin adventure, reminiscent of the quayside reception awaiting the reporter towards the end of *The Black Island*. The two heroes, who existed in reality and fiction, sat down in front of a wall hanging showing Tintin and Chang avowing their friendship and posing for a photograph in *The Blue Lotus*. Both men were overwhelmed: Hergé frail and worn out by illness; Chang robust but overcome by emotion.

ABOVE
Hergé sat down and wrote a long, deeply felt letter. Under separate cover, he sent him copies of *Tintin in Tibet* and *The Blue Lotus*.

RIGHT
With French government help and commissions, Chang works on a large bust of Hergé for Angoulême.

CHAPTER SIX **ORIENTAL ATTRACTION**

Chang and his son stayed on with Hergé and Fanny for three months until the sculptor had to return to Shanghai. While there may have been a feeling of anticlimax, since Chang still had all the energy and enthusiasm that after forty-seven years an increasingly inward-looking Hergé now lacked, for the creator of Tintin it marked the conclusion of a chapter of his life, the all-important oriental episode, two years before his death, for which it had better prepared him.

FINAL MEMENTO

For Chang, liberated from years of communist repression and hardship, it was to lead to a new life in the West. With French government help and commissions, including a large bust of Hergé for Angoulême and a portrait bust of the French president François Mitterrand, he was able to settle at Nogent-sur-Marne, outside Paris. During these later years, as a touching reminder of his friendship with Hergé, he would often wear a yellow scarf – just like Chang's, retrieved from the mountainside by Tintin in the Tibetan adventure – that Fanny had given him as a memento. He was to die at Nogent in October 1998, at the venerable age of ninety-one, a nonagenarian like his much-respected mentor and great-uncle Ma Xiangbo, and outliving Hergé by more than fifteen years. ∎

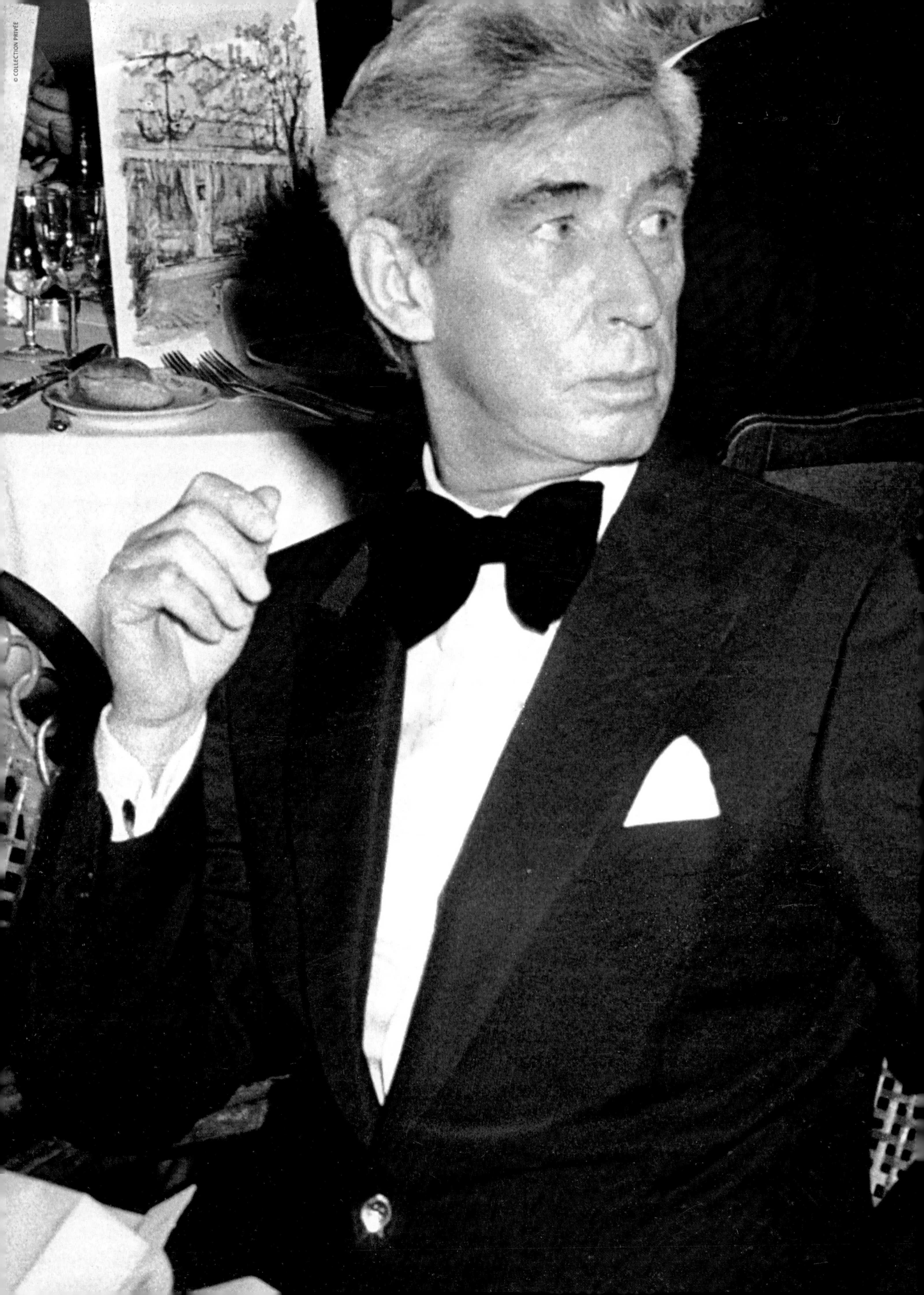

CHAPTER SEVEN

An elegant joker, with a serious side

The artist/author who created Tintin was, as one would expect, a man who saw humour everywhere, according to his friends and those who worked with him. He was a perfectionist, he could be passionate, but he liked to laugh and to make others smile. As a master of word play and repartee, and a good mimic, there was in his world a funny side to nearly everything that made the many complications and difficulties of life bearable. He was in some respects a comedian, but like many great comics he had a depressive side. It was as if he needed the humour to lift him out of such moods. 'People found it difficult to understand that he could be serious and make jokes,' Guy Dessicy, a friend for many years, recalled. 'He always kept his sense of humour, even at the end when desperately ill.'

A SERIOUS SMILE

This humour became more developed, richer and subtler with maturity. In the early Tintin adventures, and particularly the Quick and Flupke cartoons he began in *Le Petit Vingtième* on 23 January 1930, the humour was largely slapstick, as in the silent movies he went to as a boy with his mother and continued to enjoy. Quick and Flupke are two Brussels street urchins forever getting into trouble with their elders, and particularly the district policeman, for their pranks and tomfoolery. Short and pithy, limited to two pages, the cartoons yet sometimes provided a humorous gloss on serious contemporary events, such as the demagogic ranting of Adolf Hitler, or his 1934 Venice summit meeting with Benito Mussolini, the Italian fascist leader. Such examples were the nearest Hergé came to the political cartoon, but published unusually in a children's supplement.

The initial comic role in the Tintin adventures was played by Snowy, whether preening himself before a handglass at the end of the Soviet adventure or swanking to fellow hounds before setting out for Africa about the joys of lion-hunting, at which he proves unexpectedly adept. Slapstick specialists were, however, required, and came with the arrival of the Thom(p)sons in *Cigars of the Pharaoh*, indispensable in all but two of the subsequent adventures. It was the debut of Captain Haddock in 1940 in *The Crab with the Golden Claws*, and of Professor Calculus three years later in *Red Rackham's Treasure*, which really broadened the humorous aspect of the adventures. Haddock, at times so much like Hergé himself – both bon viveur and depressive – and Calculus, whose deafness and vanity are endlessly but gently made fun of, bring the humour to a new pitch, a necessary antidote to and relief from the fast-paced action. With the expanded Tintin 'family' it is worth asking which is more memorable – the humour or the actual adventure?

Certainly those who knew Hergé recall first of all his dry wit. Guy Dessicy still remembers how he told him to desist when he was helping him put his overcoat on, saying it was difficult enough for one person to struggle with it, let alone two. Which is a true enough observation,

ABOVE
1934 Venice summit meeting with Benito Mussolini.

LEFT
People found it difficult to understand that he could be serious and make jokes.

worthy of an impatient Captain Haddock. The regular and obligatory afternoon teatime he instituted in the studios was an occasion for his assistants to down pens and brushes and drink tea from fine porcelain while the master emerged to exchange pleasantries and jokes. The pleasure he clearly derived from the jokes he wove into the adventures contribute enormously to their enjoyment.

CODED MEANINGS

One source of delight to him was to use his knowledge of Marollien, the Brussels dialect he knew from his maternal grandmother, as the basis for some of the names of places or characters, particularly Arabs, or for a fictional foreign language such as Syldavian. It worked wonderfully, as the native of Brussels could spot and relish the origin, while others would admire its originality. It served as a bonus for those in the know, adding another dimension of appreciation. Some of these subtleties are lost in translation into other languages, but the best of the translators – and generally standards are high – try to capture them as far as possible.

In spite of his ultra-conventional background and upbringing, or perhaps because of it, Hergé was happily unconventional and completely open minded, unlike many of his contemporaries. This enabled him to be thoroughly modern, or 'with it' to use a term of the 1960s – an iconoclastic and liberating decade with which, unlike others of his generation, he felt particularly comfortable. It also meant that he could communicate wonderfully with young people, an obvious strength for a children's author. His fascination for modern art and contemporary music only accelerated with advancing years; he progressed enthusiastically from the Italian Futurism and Russian Suprematism that excited him as a young man to Andy Warhol, pop art and the abstract paintings of Mark Rothko; from Schubert and Debussy to the Beatles and Pink Floyd. In the early 1970s he sent his close friends Guy and Léona Dessicy to London to see *Jesus Christ Superstar* and gave them the LP of the musical.

BELOW LEFT
In these intriguing drawings of the *Alph-Art*, Haddock seems to have become a pipe-smoking apostle of 'flower power'.

BELOW RIGHT
Hergé felt particularly comfortable communicating with young people, an obvious strength for a children's author.

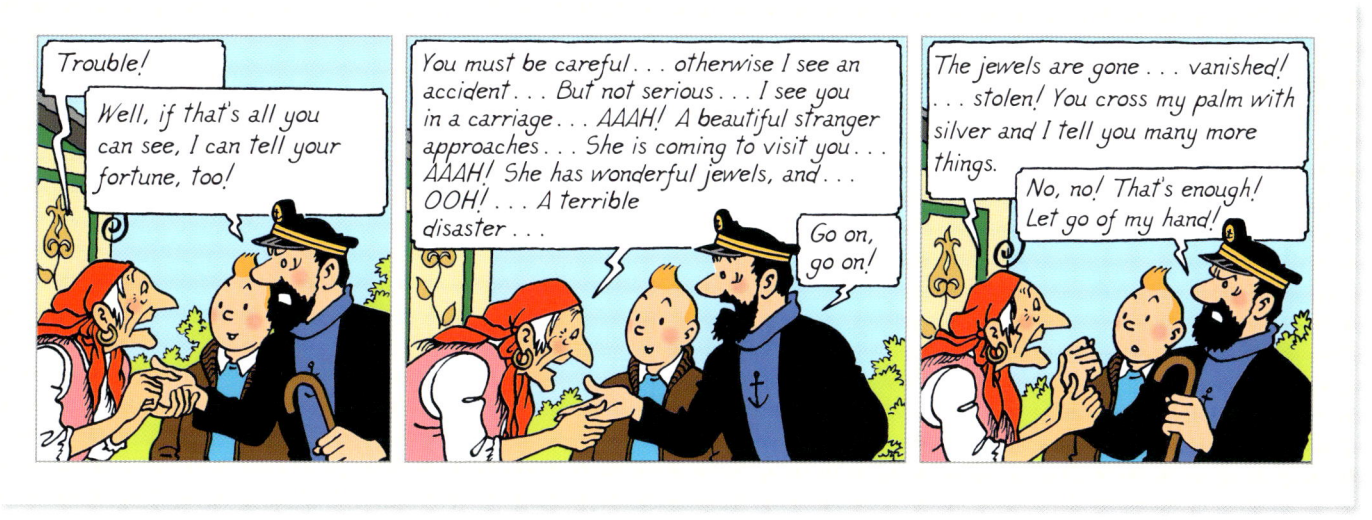

CHAPTER SEVEN **AN ELEGANT JOKER, WITH A SERIOUS SIDE**

> **Panel 1:**
> Trouble!
> Well, if that's all you can see, I can tell your fortune, too!
>
> **Panel 2:**
> You must be careful... otherwise I see an accident... But not serious... I see you in a carriage... AAAH! A beautiful stranger approaches... She is coming to visit you... AAAH! She has wonderful jewels, and... OOH!... A terrible disaster...
> Go on, go on!
>
> **Panel 3:**
> The jewels are gone... vanished! ... stolen! You cross my palm with silver and I tell you many more things.
> No, no! That's enough! Let go of my hand!

He was fascinated by fortune-telling and kept in touch with a clairvoyant, which gives added relevance to the scene at the beginning of *The Castafiore Emerald*.

Terrible nightmares and witchcraft feature in *The Seven Crystal Balls* and its sequel, *Prisoners of the Sun*.

It was the same with his interest in psychology, as well as Eastern philosophies and religions, subjects on which he would read voraciously. He had, unusually for one born in 1907, a 'New Age' mentality which became very clear in some of the later Tintin adventures, such as *Tintin in Tibet*, with its handling of dreams and extrasensory perception, *Flight 714*, with its inclusion of extra-terrestrial influences, and particularly the unfinished *Tintin and Alph-Art*, which deals with the world of contemporary art, forgeries and a Bhagwan-inspired sect. While at the start of *Tintin and the Picaros* the reporter arrives at Marlinspike sporting a nuclear disarmament emblem on his motorcycle helmet, amid the undeveloped sketches for *Tintin and Alph-Art* one finds Captain Haddock, who has taken up painting, wearing beads and a kaftan. Something amazing has happened: Haddock has become a beatnik, or hippy. He has grown his hair long, wears John Lennon-type spectacles, strums the guitar – as Hergé himself enjoyed doing – and adds generously flared embroidered trousers and a tasselled shoulder bag to his wardrobe. In these intriguing drawings, he seems to have become a pipe-smoking apostle of 'flower power'.

Hergé would keep a notebook by his bed, not only to note ideas for use in Tintin but also to record what he could remember of his dreams for their possible interpretation. Dreams and dream sequences are to be found throughout *The Adventures of Tintin*. Terrible nightmares and witchcraft feature in *The Seven Crystal Balls* and its sequel, *Prisoners of the Sun*, where the explorers are struck down one by one, falling into comas and having fits when their doll-like effigies are tortured by the Inca high priest – the price for their violation of the Inca tombs. The apparent curse smacks of the voodoo practised in certain parts of Africa and Haiti, about which Hergé would have read. There is already an incidence of witchcraft or juju and a fetish in *Tintin in the Congo*.

He was fascinated by fortune-telling and kept in touch with a clairvoyant, which gives added relevance to the scene at the beginning of *The Castafiore Emerald* where the old gypsy woman tries to read a reluctant Captain Haddock's palm. Earlier Madame Yamilah had stunned the music hall with her revelations at the beginning of *The Seven Crystal Balls*. It was a clairvoyant acquaintance who persuaded Hergé to take down the Jacques Van Melkebeke portrait of him as a young man from its prominent position at his home because of its 'negative impulses'. His susceptibility to such influences demonstrated his openness to ideas, however unconventional.

TELLING FORTUNES

He was keenly interested in astrology and horoscopes, attaching great importance to the fact that, with a date of birth of 22 May, his sign of the zodiac was Gemini, the heavenly twins, the constellation Castor and Pollux. This, he believed, could account for certain characteristics and behaviour. Friends found two sides to his nature: one natural and spontaneous, the other reserved and shy. He could be as frivolous and happy as he could wise and earnest. The fact that he shared the same birthday (though not year) with Raymond Leblanc, responsible for reviving his fortunes by establishing *Tintin* magazine in September 1946, was certainly significant to him. Observant readers will note that the carnival procession on page 54 of *Tintin and the Picaros*, with its various references to the world of strip cartoons, including Mickey Mouse* and Astérix**, proceeds appropriately down the Calle de 22 Mayo (the Avenue of 22 May), a fitting celebration of his birthday.

Hypnotism was another area he eagerly explored and brought into the Tintin adventures more than once. Already in *Cigars of the Pharaoh*, the evil fakir provides an example of his hypnotic skills when he 'programmes' the Egyptologist Sophocles Sarcophagus to kill Tintin, and then mesmerises the reporter, causing him to swoon and drop his pistol.

CHAPTER SEVEN **AN ELEGANT JOKER, WITH A SERIOUS SIDE**

ABOVE
Observant readers will note that the carnival procession on page 54 of *Tintin and the Picaros* proceeds down the Calle de 22 Mayo, a fitting celebration of his birthday.

RIGHT
In *The Seven Crystal Balls,* Ragdalam, the fakir, puts Madame Yamilah into a hypnotic trance.

In the music hall scene of *The Seven Crystal Balls*, there is Ragdalam the fakir, who puts Madame Yamilah 'into a hypnotic trance'. Much later, in *Flight 714*, a form of hypnotism is exercised by Mik Kanrokitoff, the enigmatic character who emerges towards the end of the adventure and was based on Jacques Bergier, the writer, television personality and co-founder of the magazine *Planète*, to which Hergé was an avid subscriber. He had been impressed by Bergier's book *Le Matin des magiciens*, published in Paris by Gallimard in 1960, in which he wrote about contacts with extraterrestrial beings and examined references in religious texts to 'interplanetary vessels'. Similarly Hergé had been riveted by a book published seven years later by Robert Charroux, *Le Livre des maîtres du monde*, which described prehistoric depictions of cosmonauts from outer space. Charroux had earlier highlighted allusions in religious writing to 'flying chariots' and 'winged discs'. Meanwhile Jung, whom Hergé admired so much, had in his last book, *A Modern Myth*, given a psychological interpretation to the phenomenon of flying saucers.

Hergé's intellectual curiosity was matched by his extreme visual awareness, an invaluable asset for an artist. His eyes were always searching, noting and recalling. A then young employee at his publisher Casterman recalls his first meeting with Hergé when he started outlining a proposition but was suddenly cut short and asked about the striking coloured checks of his shirt. It is no wonder that even the most minor character in *The Adventures of Tintin* is meticulously and appropriately dressed. Take any crowd scene from an adventure and note the variety of detail: there is nothing routine about filling in a background. Although this was inevitably painstaking work that took time, even with the later help of the studios, it resulted in a decor and background that were full of life and animation, much as in a filmed scene.

LEFT
Dreams and dream sequences are to be found throughout *The Adventures of Tintin*.

---

* He encountered just such a Mickey Mouse at Disneyland, Florida, on a visit in 1972. Walt Disney's famous creation first appeared in November 1928, just two months before Tintin.

** At one point – towards the end of 1966 – Hergé considered the plucky Gaul created by René Goscinny and Albert Uderzo to be a real rival to Tintin and rose to the challenge by embarking on Flight 714.

ELEGANTLY ATTIRED

Hergé himself attached great importance to dress and was invariably immaculately turned out, influenced most certainly by his father's profession as a boys' outfitter. Photographs of him during the 1930s show him elegantly suited, often with a trilby or fedora hat and with careful attention to accessories. His was an undoubtedly debonair appearance. There may have been some of Tintin in it, if not necessarily the plus fours, but also the well-attired Haddock we find in the pages of *The Seven Crystal Balls*, where, thanks to the generosity of Professor Calculus and Tintin's discovery of Red Rackham's treasure, he has been able to acquire his ancestral home of Marlinspike Hall. There Haddock, like Hergé at the time, is very much an adherent of *le style anglais*, with grey flannel trousers, tweed jacket and well-chosen silk ties. During the late 1950s, when Hergé would visit London for meetings with his English publisher Methuen, he would set aside an afternoon for shopping in Jermyn Street for shirts, ties and hosiery, and sometimes jackets and trousers. Dress was part of his Anglophilia. His style, his second wife Fanny remembers, was '*très* gentleman' ('very much the gentleman'). Fanny recounts that later, however, during the 1970s, his taste became more Italianate, and on their regular trips there he would purchase shoes and fine cotton socks. The change is reflected in *The Adventures of Tintin*, for this was the time when the reporter finally – and in the opinion of many, including to some extent Hergé himself, mistakenly – replaced his ubiquitous plus fours with more modish jeans.

Haddock, like Hergé at the time, is very much an adherent of *le style anglais*, with grey flannel trousers, tweed jacket and well-chosen silk ties.

CHAPTER SEVEN **AN ELEGANT JOKER, WITH A SERIOUS SIDE**

Hergé's inquisitiveness made him a difficult subject to interview, quite apart from the fact that he scorned personal publicity. Despite his early and successful work in advertising, he was certainly no self-publicist. He was by nature remarkably modest and unassuming. Often, instead of answering questions, he would ask them back with a skill that many a politician could envy. There are comparatively few interviews of consequence, the principal being Numa Sadoul's breakthrough in persuading him to sit down and be interviewed over a period of time in conversations that were recorded on tape. Sadoul's youth, enthusiasm and exotic background clearly appealed to him. The transcript was duly returned to Hergé, who subjected it to long and heavy vetting. This finally resulted in a publication, *Entretiens avec Hergé* (Interviews with Hergé), which is the nearest we have to an autobiography. It is far from frank and frequently evasive, but nevertheless of considerable interest. For most, though not all, of the time, the presence of a microphone led to him playing his cards even closer to his chest than usual. In recent years passages cut by Hergé have been reinstated, resulting in a fuller account that provides more information and demonstrates the artist's concern for the projection of his image.

For this there was without doubt good reason. Already a sensitive person by nature, he had suffered enormously as a result of the aspersions to which he was subjected immediately after the war for his continuation of Tintin in *Le Soir*, Belgium's leading daily newspaper which was taken over by the German occupiers as a propaganda organ. He felt that accusations of collaboration were grossly unfair and hurtful and, to a remarkable extent for the creator of such a public figure as Tintin, withdrew into himself, shunning publicity and falling back on a small circle of trusted friends. Guy Dessicy recalls how 'he never talked politics' and was 'very discreet'. He was deeply wounded by all the troubles he had incurred as a result of what he saw as his patriotism. Raymond Leblanc too remembers him being 'very reserved, except sometimes with friends'.

An idealist in his youth like Tintin, Hergé had seen many illusions shattered by the war and its aftermath, and he emerged with an uncharacteristic streak of bitterness and disappointment. Now he was more like Haddock, whom he had introduced in 1940 as the necessary counterpoint to the too-perfect Tintin. Haddock, like Hergé, could be moody, morose and even depressive, as readers discover on page 50 of *The Seven Crystal Balls*, when Tintin arrives at Marlinspike and is told by the concerned butler Nestor that the captain has 'aged ten years since this trouble began'. He finds the once ebullient captain slumped dejectedly in an elegant wing chair, still in his dressing gown and pyjamas. It was this sequence which marked the resumption in 1946 of the adventure – in *Tintin* magazine – after its abrupt interruption with the closure of the wartime *Le Soir* in 1944.

BELOW RIGHT
Haddock, like Hergé, could be moody, morose and even depressive as on page 50 of *The Seven Crystal Balls* when Tintin finds the captain in dressing gown and pyjamas.

LEFT
Sketches for strips in *Le Soir*.

THE ADVENTURES OF HERGÉ, CREATOR OF TINTIN

Hergé launched his own advertising studio – Atelier Hergé – eliciting a wide range of requests to which he responded with sometimes superb examples of publicity such as those for Brussels' leading department store.

Only too aware of the political storm clouds that were massing in May 1940, it became clear that the life of Hergé and millions of others would be turned upside down.

SUCCESSFUL YEARS

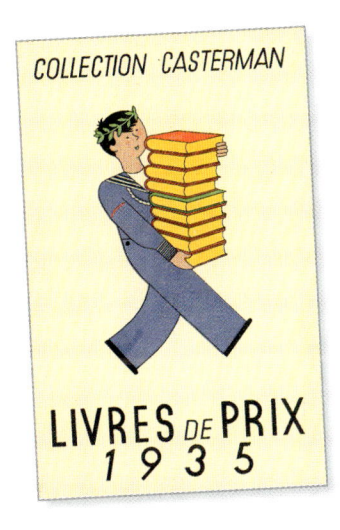

For Hergé the pre-war years were full of optimism and acclaim. From his first steps in January 1929, Tintin had been a runaway success. A year later he won further plaudits with the Quick and Flupke cartoons. Hergé had established himself as a sought-after illustrator with as many commissions as he could fulfil. While continuing his newspaper work, he launched his own advertising studio – Atelier Hergé – eliciting a wide range of requests to which he responded with sometimes superb examples of publicity, for Brussels' leading department stores, biscuit and chocolate makers, breweries and fashion houses. To add to the other feathers in his cap, Belgium's most prestigious publisher, Casterman, who initially employed him to design book covers and as an illustrator, was now publishing his own books. As was evident in the Tintin adventures of the time, however, and some of the Quick and Flupke cartoons, he was only too aware of the political storm clouds that were massing. He also had a role to play as an army reservist, a lieutenant liable to be called to arms.

When the long-brewing storm finally broke in September 1939 with the blitzkrieg of Poland by the Nazis, leading to the strange wait of the phoney war and then, for a second time in the century, the brutal invasion by the Germans of Belgium and France in May 1940, it became clear that the life of Hergé and millions of others would be turned upside down.

Always a staunch royalist, he was among the first to heed King Léopold III's call following the fall of Belgium for Belgians to return to work and keep the country going. Léopold's stand may have been purely patriotic, but he would have been better advised to follow the example of other ousted European royals and his own government and choose a London exile, rather than allow himself to be held under house arrest by the Germans at his palace of Laeken. That and the fact that, as commander-in-chief, he had surrendered to the advancing Germans as Belgian casualties mounted without first consulting the Allies were long held against him, leading to acute controversy and his abdication after the war – in 1951 – in favour of his son Baudouin. Hergé, not surprisingly, felt that Léopold had like himself been treated unfairly. Always a loyal subject, he took pleasure in meeting him after the war in his Swiss exile and going fishing with the former monarch on Lake Geneva. Hergé would have preferred, however, to have followed Tintin's example in *King Ottokar's Sceptre* and saved the throne for him.

The Catholic *Le Vingtième Siècle* had closed down with the German capture of Brussels. There was no place for a Catholic Church newspaper under the Nazis. All at once, and for the first time, Hergé was jobless and Tintin without an audience. He was, however, quickly offered employment and a new home for Tintin by *Le Soir*, Belgium's leading daily, then and now, commanding a circulation much higher than any Tintin had been used to. Hergé was asked to create a children's supplement, as he had so successfully for *Le Vingtième Siècle*, to be called *Le Soir Jeunesse*, with Tintin as its mainstay and coming out, like its model, on Thursdays. It was an offer he felt he could not refuse, yet there was a large fly in the ointment – the fact that the newspaper came under Nazi control, causing its critics to rename it *Le Soir volé* (the stolen *Soir*).

A DELICATE CHOICE

Hergé's view may have been that it was important to continue Tintin, if only to keep up the spirits of the Belgian people during the grim realities of occupation, something he had experienced as a boy in the 1914–18 war. He also likened it to the necessary menial tasks performed by miners, bakers and tram drivers in keeping the country going. He was, furthermore, following the king's call to work. There is no doubt, moreover, that Tintin was appreciated more than ever during those dark days. While paper shortages gradually reduced the scale of the Tintin strip –

Casterman, who initially employed Hergé to design book covers and as an illustrator, was now publishing his own books.

Hergé considered it was important to continue Tintin, if only to keep up the spirits of the Belgian people during the grim realities of occupation.

after a while *Le Soir Jeunesse* had fewer pages, before having to be abandoned altogether, with Tintin transferred to the main newspaper, enjoying an unhappy proximity with reports of Wehrmacht successes and other propaganda – Casterman found it could sell as many of the books as it could print. There was definitely a demand for distraction which was well fulfilled by the adventures produced during the war years: *The Crab with the Golden Claws*, *The Shooting Star*, *The Secret of the Unicorn* and *Red Rackham's Treasure*, and the equivalent of about fifty book pages of *The Seven Crystal Balls*. Wisely, Hergé moved away from adventures reflecting current affairs – in 1940 he broke off a story of sabotage and international crisis, *Land of Black Gold*, which he had begun in 1939 and was to resume in 1948, at the point where the German villain Müller leaves Tintin to die in the desert – to non-political stories of drug trafficking, scientific expeditions, treasure hunts and mysterious curses. These were exciting but, unlike some of the pre-war adventures, uncontroversial, just what readers and editors wanted.

This working arrangement ended abruptly, however, with the British liberation of Brussels on 3 September 1944, led by the tanks of the Guards Armoured Division. *Le Soir volé* was shut down, purged and reopened with a completely new, uncompromised team. Its entire previous staff, from the most strident propagandists and worst apologists of collaboration to the most harmless cartoonists and crossword compilers, were banned from further work and subject to investigation. There was an impatience to settle old scores from which Hergé did not escape: four times he was arrested by various militia or paramilitary groups, suffering the indignity of spending one night in a crowded prison cell, before being released. Tintin may have been popular but his popularity was not enough to keep Hergé above suspicion. There were some who were jealous of his success and there were others, as in many a Tintin adventure, who sought his downfall.

In 1940 Hergé breaks off a story of sabotage and international crisis, *Land of Black Gold*, at the point where the German villain Müller leaves Tintin to die in the desert.

CHAPTER SEVEN **AN ELEGANT JOKER, WITH A SERIOUS SIDE**

SMEARS

His detractors tried to link him to the 'Rexist' Belgian fascist party, led by Léon Degrelle, who had worked for *Le Vingtième Siècle* when Hergé joined the newspaper after leaving school. It was in the newspapers that Degrelle sent back to *Le Vingtième Siècle* from Mexico, where he was on assignment, that Hergé discovered and was inspired by American strip cartoons. Furthermore, Hergé had provided illustrations for at least one book of Degrelle's, *L'Histoire de la guerre scolaire* (The Story of the Scholastic War), which was published in 1932. Degrelle then and later, moreover, declared himself to be, like thousands of other Belgians, a great admirer of Tintin and Hergé's work. There is no evidence, however, that Degrelle was more than an acquaintance, or that Hergé shared any of his radically pro-German views. On the contrary, the more vociferous Degrelle became, the farther Hergé distanced himself from any association. He emphatically, and very wisely, turned down an offer to work for the official Rexist magazine or become the illustrator of the movement, which welcomed the arrival of the Nazis and was at the forefront of collaboration, even helping to raise a Walloon Waffen-SS regiment to send to the Russian front to fight alongside a similar Flemish 'Legion'.

Degrelle, who could very well have been at the back of Hergé's mind as a fifth columnist – a model for the leader of the Iron Guard – when he was working on *King Ottokar's Sceptre*, became a favourite of Hitler, who referred to him as 'the son I wish I had'. Following the liberation of Belgium, he managed to escape justice and execution, fleeing to Franco's Spain, where he lived comfortably, a committed fascist to the end, until his death in April 1994 at the age of eighty-seven.

In the turbulent days of September 1944, when retribution was sought against any who had given support to the Nazi occupiers, with little discrimination, a publication, *Galerie des Traitres* (Gallery of Traitors), was circulated, listing those who had worked on *Le Soir volé*. Hergé's name appears twice – once misspelled as Remy instead of Remi – with his date of birth and address. The entries are inconclusive and truly Tintinesque – straight out of an adventure such as *King Ottokar's Sceptre*. The first declares: 'According to certain information received, was a Rexist, but we have not been able to obtain confirmation.' The second, after noting that he worked for the wartime *Le Soir*, added: 'Impossible to obtain information on this individual. All that we know is that he must be watched closely.' Hergé, not surprisingly, felt very threatened – he even feared for his physical safety – and deeply hurt at being branded a traitor when he was passionately patriotic about his country and had given ample proof of this in his work.

There was no substance to any of the charges and no case for him to answer, though as an interested spectator he did attend some of the tribunals where culpable former colleagues and friends from *Le Soir* were tried and severely punished; some were given stiff prison terms, others even sentenced to death by firing squad. There were also those who chose to avoid the process and escaped to live in other countries, particularly France. Hergé's apparently innocuous link with the newspaper had cost him dearly, for when mud is thrown some of it will always stick. Although a continuation of newspaper work was for the time being impossible, he did at least have a foundation on which to rebuild: his work for Casterman, involving the continued recasting of the pre-war black-and-white Tintin books into the new sixty-two-page colour format he had devised with the publisher. 'Casterman gave him continuity during and after the war,' according to Guy Dessicy.

The recasting of the black-and-white Tintin books
into colour gave Hergé continued work.

119

REVIVAL

It was the young businessman Raymond Blanc, however, with his commendable record of wartime resistance, who at this crucial stage did the most to get Hergé and Tintin back on track and into production by offering to set up a weekly magazine for young people to be called *Tintin*. Since his teens – his mother subscribed to *Le Vingtième Siècle* – Leblanc had been captivated by the ace reporter of *Le Petit Vingtième* and, aged sixteen, had gone as far as travelling from his home in the Ardennes to Brussels especially to greet Tintin at the Gare du Nord on his return from the Congo in 1931. Having distinguished himself in the war, during which, like thousands of others, he continued to follow Tintin in *Le Soir* despite its associations, Leblanc quickly proved himself an entrepreneur with flair in its aftermath, launching a number of highly profitable business ventures.

The Tintin project was the most personal, for he was keen to see the reporter back in action, and though he did not yet know Hergé he was eager to champion his cause. For Hergé, his endorsement by Leblanc and his circle was the best way of silencing his enemies. 'He had done nothing bad – perhaps it was a mistake to continue to have the stories published – but he never betrayed anyone, never fought and never did Belgium any wrong,' Leblanc maintained then and repeated in an interview sixty years later. His supportive stand clearly helped Hergé obtain the certificate of good citizenship that was necessary for him to resume journalism. With his business connections Leblanc was assured of the plant and the necessary paper – still in very short supply – and with some friends he raised the capital to launch the magazine. Leblanc, who had already started a romantic publication, *Cœur*, and a cinema magazine, *Ciné-Sélection*, was confident that this publishing venture would succeed, as he had not a shadow of doubt about Tintin's popularity. 'Tintin', Leblanc could state with as much certainty in 2006 as in 1946, 'was a magic word.'

His first meeting with Hergé came towards the end of 1945 following his demobilisation in June after serving as a liaison officer at Field Marshal Bernard Montgomery's headquarters. Recalling that encounter more than sixty years later, he said the initial surprise came when 'a young smiling man, likeable from the first moment' entered the room – he had imagined Monsieur Hergé, as he, like other readers, knew him, to be much older. In fact, at thirty-eight the creator of Tintin was only eight years older than Leblanc.

BELOW LEFT
Leblanc obtains the necessary certificates of good citizenship for Hergé in May 1946.

BELOW RIGHT
Leblanc standing proudly in front of the model of the *Tintin* building. Its famous emblem could be seen for miles around (above).

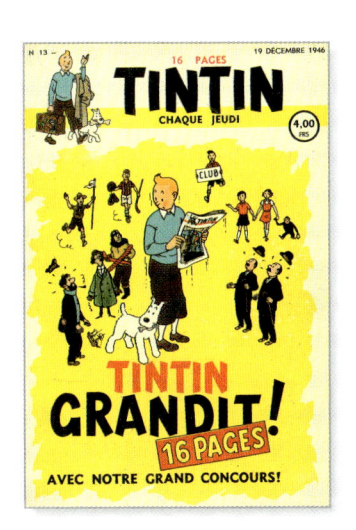

CHAPTER SEVEN **AN ELEGANT JOKER, WITH A SERIOUS SIDE**

Tintin magazine was, like everything the reporter had previously been associated with, a triumph. 19 December 1946 issue.

Eagerly awaiting the first issue of *Tintin* magazine *Au Petit Constructeur*, 26 September 1946.

Jacobs, Van Melkebeke and Hergé at Watermael-Boitsfort, 1940s.

At that first encounter, Leblanc remembers him being 'warm but worried'. When he broached his idea of establishing a *Tintin* magazine, Hergé doubted that he would be allowed to resume work. He was greatly shocked by the war and the mood of recrimination and revenge that had set in. Leblanc undertook to help him obtain the necessary certificate of good citizenship, which duly arrived in May 1946, allowing the plan to proceed and *Tintin* magazine to be launched on 26 September 1946, with Hergé as its artistic director and Leblanc its publisher. Hergé's friend and portraitist Jacques Van Melkebeke was its first editor, and he was able to include a number of his associates in the team. The magazine was made up initially of a dozen pages; Hergé was given the double centre-page spread in colour for Tintin, with others sharing the remaining space. He would take it in turns with his colleagues to design the cover. The Brussels trams carried new advertisements that reminded Belgians of comforting old habits: 'Read Tintin, Every Thursday!' ('*Lisez Tintin, chaque jeudi!*') – publicity that was repeated in all cinemas. Tintin, meanwhile, would resume his quest to unravel the mystery of *The Seven Crystal Balls* and rescue Professor Calculus from his kidnappers, which had been broken off abruptly with the closure of the wartime *Le Soir*.

Just as there could be no doubt about Hergé's aesthetic judgement, so there could be none about Leblanc's business acumen. He rightly sensed that it was a boom time for publishers with a post-war public desperate for distraction, overcoming Hergé's reservations that the market for young readers might already have been saturated. *Tintin* magazine was, like everything the reporter had previously been associated with, a triumph, with weekly circulation quickly reaching an impressive 100,000 copies. It had been the same when Tintin began his adventures in January 1929 in *Le Petit Vingtième*, which suddenly saw its circulation soar. There was similar success when Casterman took over publication of the books, while *Le Soir* predictably benefited from the launch of *Le Soir Jeunesse*. Tintin, if not Hergé, had the Midas touch.

TENSIONS

Tintin magazine was to prove unexpectedly durable, carrying on for thirty years to include the last completed adventure, *Tintin and the Picaros* (1976), but the partnership could at times be difficult. Though a solid friendship developed, the consummate artist could not always agree with the astute businessman. Hergé found after a while that the weekly production of a double page, a requirement he had not had to meet since the days of *Le Petit Vingtième*, was very demanding, indeed exhausting. Furthermore, Leblanc was doubtful about the merits of one or two of Hergé's appointments, while the artist resented the attempted imposition of artists and later editors by Leblanc, feeling that, as artistic director, he should have complete control of all such appointments. Yet it was Leblanc who was to display great patience during the early 1950s, when Hergé, on the brink of a complete nervous collapse, found he could work no more. Already before the war he had broken out into severe eczema and burst into boils when Tintin's tight deadlines put him under pressure, and now, with his marriage additionally under severe strain, the situation was potentially much worse.

Twice during this period of crisis Hergé suddenly disappeared without telling friends or colleagues: once for six weeks in 1949, the second time in 1950 for more than a year. He sought refuge mostly in Switzerland, where, by Lake Geneva, he tried to find peace and an escape from the pressures of life in Brussels, at work and at home. He always had a great yearning for calm. During part of his absence he went camping with his close friend Marcel Dehaye, reliving the scouting expeditions of his youth.

Leblanc, meanwhile, was left with a *Tintin* magazine without Tintin, its *raison d'être*. Like the magazine's many readers in Belgium, and now in France, he felt frustrated and disappointed. On the first occasion, through the good offices of Hergé's first wife Germaine, he was able to bring him back to resume *Land of Black Gold*, with apologies to readers and a humorous drawing. The second time was more difficult and Germaine was not necessarily the solution, for she was part of the problem. Always loyal to Hergé, Hergée, as he had called her in younger days, was, in the opinion of some of their friends, too maternal, fussing over him constantly, as Castafiore was to over the wheelchair-bound Captain Haddock in *The Castafiore Emerald*. They had met at *Le Vingtième Siècle*, where she had been the secretary of the forceful Father Wallez, who did so much not only to promote Hergé's early career but also their match, and were duly married on 20 July 1932. She was a considerable support to him, especially during the difficult years of the war and its aftermath, but during the 1950s the relationship became fraught, with frequent rows and Hergé's absences and occasional friendships with other women, which caused him tremendous remorse afterwards.

CHAPTER SEVEN **AN ELEGANT JOKER, WITH A SERIOUS SIDE**

ABOVE RIGHT
The *Tintin* team. Caricature of Hergé slaving at his desk, *Tintin* magazine.

LEFT
Cover of *Tintin* magazine, 27 October 1949, where Hergé makes his apologies to readers through this humorous drawing.

Hergé seeks refuge with friends Charlie and Line Fornara by Lake Geneva. He dedicated two books to them.

They had not managed to have children, which may, according to friends, have been the result of radiotherapy treatment he had received for an ailment. His younger brother Paul and his wife Jeannot had two children, Georges and Denise, fulfilling their role, like Mr and Mrs Legrand in *The Adventures of Jo, Zette and Jocko*, as the ideal post-war family unit. Hergé had been asked by his French publisher to provide adventures that were more family oriented than Tintin, and the Legrands were his answer – the father a civil engineer, the mother a housewife, and the family completed by the brother and sister Jo and Zette with their pet chimpanzee Jocko. It was a charming sideline from Tintin but lacked its depth and therefore its broad appeal. Although Hergé could communicate so wonderfully with children in his work, and his own attitude to life could have a childish innocence and enthusiasm, he was not, according to all accounts, particularly comfortable in the presence of children and was not a model uncle as far as Georges and Denise were concerned.

It was pages taken from *The Adventures of Jo, Zette and Jocko* and recycled Quick and Flupke cartoons which filled the gap left by Tintin during Hergé's absence without leave. Hergé's plea of exhaustion did little to appease the demands on Leblanc of Georges Dargaud, *Tintin* magazine's publisher in France, who found it understandably absurd to publish it without Tintin. Finally, after a break of eighteen months, Hergé and Tintin returned to the magazine, but the relations between artist and publisher could never be the same again.

Hergé soldiered on, more independent of Leblanc, having established his own studios in April 1950 in the Avenue Louise with his hand-picked team of artists and assistants. The move reflected one made in the 1930s, when he won the right to work more congenially at home than at the offices of *Le Vingtième Siècle*. Now he was asserting his independence by moving from Leblanc at the Rue du Lombard to the especially created Studios Hergé. It was hoped that in his own environment, with his own personnel, he would find it easier, indeed possible, to continue Tintin. The continual demands of Tintin meant that creation was not always a labour of love, and there remains the image – which he drew for *Tintin* magazine in 1947 – of Hergé slaving at his desk, supervised by a figure of Tintin holding a martinet.

123

ROMANCE AND TRUE LOVE

The sequel and the final chapter of Hergé's life was to begin in the studios one fine day at the end of June 1955, when a very spoiled young girl, according to her own account, arrived there after a projected trip to Italy with a girlfriend did not come off. She had seen an advertisement in *Le Soir* for a colourist, applied and after two interviews was offered the job, her first. When she arrived on a Friday, she remembers, she panicked and almost did not go in. Fanny Vlamynck, an only child from a well-off family, was not quite twenty-one years old, had discovered Tintin between the ages of seven and ten, and was interested in fashion drawings and design. Like Raymond Leblanc at his first meeting with him ten years earlier, she imagined Hergé to be much older than the trim forty-eight-year-old she encountered. It was not quite love at first sight; first it was work, and she remembers joining the team that was at the time producing *The Calculus Affair*, one of Hergé's most inspired adventures. Her job as a colourist meant that she had to make sure that exactly the same colours and tones were maintained throughout the plates. She recalls vividly the regular 4 p.m. teatime when Hergé would emerge with Bob De Moor, by then his right-hand assistant, and for a quarter or half an hour 'would exchange jokes and tell a great many stories'.

During the summer of 1958, Hergé and Bob De Moor went off together to make some sketches aboard ship and suddenly, Fanny recalls, 'I felt this frightful void or absence because he was not there… I discovered this feeling. But I knew he was married and never for a moment thought that there could be anything.' Then that November at All Saints, she knocked at his door to say goodbye before leaving for her drawing evening class. 'He was at his desk still busy working under the light of the lamp before the long holiday weekend. The others had gone. He insisted on going down with me and we took the lift together. He said how long the weekend would be without me. And I replied that it would be for me too. "Don't say that! Don't say that!" he answered. And oh! I was bowled over.' It was the beginning of a great and unexpected romance, unlike anything to be found in *The Adventures of Tintin*, which as it developed was to lift Hergé from his bouts of depression, finally vanquished as he worked on *Tintin in Tibet*, the adventure of friendship. It allowed the unalloyed domestic comedy of *The Castafiore Emerald*, the only adventure in which Tintin travels nowhere and yet one of the best. It reflected how content Hergé had become in his private life through his relationship with Fanny. *The Adventures of Tintin* could well have satisfactorily concluded there, allowing the adventures of Hergé to have a happy ending as he finally enjoyed a respite and could begin to do just some of the travelling his reporter had managed over the years. Tintin, however, could not be sacrificed so easily and would continue, if at a more leisurely pace, to Hergé's end.

By the summer of 1960, Hergé and Fanny were living together. In due course her parents' initial opposition to the match, and reservations over an age difference of more than twenty-seven years, were overcome. Age, as any Tintin reader knows, is immaterial. How old is Tintin? Fanny stopped working and they set up house together. The unthinkable had happened.

Germaine felt betrayed and there were inevitably recriminations. Hergé's innate sense of loyalty made divorce from her difficult – they would remain friends and he made a point of trying to see her every Monday – but eventually its formal promulgation came at the end of March 1977, and on 23 May, a day after Hergé's seventieth birthday, Fanny became his second wife. She saw herself as Madame Remi – rather than Madame Hergé, as Germaine had – and there was always a clear distinction between his work and home.

THE LEGACY

It was to be Fanny who looked after Georges as his strength ebbed in the six years of life left him, and it was to be Fanny on whose shoulders the considerable responsibility of safeguarding his heritage – *The Adventures of Tintin* – would fall when the adventures of Hergé closed on 3 March 1983. Nearly thirty years later this was to culminate in the opening of the Hergé Museum at Louvain-la-Neuve, just outside Brussels, a goal and a tribute Fanny had long sought to realise. Tintin's enduring popularity would ensure that the memory of his creator – a charming, courteous man who hated vulgarity and bad manners, and had a life-enhancing sense of humour – would live on. ■

The sequel and the final chapter of Hergé's life was to begin in the studios one fine day at the end of June 1955.

LEFT PAGE
Hergé and Fanny on their travels.

RIGHT
Hergé and Fanny on holiday.

Index

A Académie des Beaux-Arts, Brussels 89, 94, 95 • Ainsworth Means, Philip 56 • Albers, Josef 40 • Aldrin, Buzz 66 • Alechinsky, Pierre 5 • Allen, Woody 69 • Appel, Karel 5 • Arbuckle, 'Fattie' 63 • Armstrong, Neil 7, 66, 85, 101 • Arnould, Marcel 35

B Baden-Powell, Agnes 75 • Baden-Powell, Robert, Lord 75, 77, 81, 87 • Balla, Giacomo 33, 34 • Balzac, Honoré de 66 • Barret, André 72 • Barthelness, Richard 67 • Baudouin, King of Belgium 117 • Bauhaus 40 • BBC 62 • Beatles, the 66, 110 • Beery, Wallace 67 • Beethoven, Ludwig van 66 • Belvision 71, 72 • Bergier, Jacques 113 • Bertoia, Harry 36 • Black Elk 19 • Boccioni, Umberto 33 • Bon Marché, department store 14 • Bosch, Hieronymus 39 • Botticelli, Sandro 7 • Bouise, Jean 72 • Boxer Rising 90 • Braque, Georges 33, 35 • Brel, Jacques 66 • Bruegel, Pieter 39 • Buchan, John 25, 65

C Caballé, Montserrat 66 • Caesar, Julius 9 • Calder, Alexander 36, 37 • Callas, Maria 66 • Campbell, Sir Malcolm 61 • Capone, Al 48, 66 • Carrefour Gallery 34, 38, 39 • Carroll, Madeleine 65 • Casterman, publisher 7, 13, 40, 49, 55, 72, 73, 113, 117, 118, 119, 121 • Centre Pompidou, Paris 5, 51 • César (César Baldaccini) 34, 35 • Cézanne, Paul 33 • Chang Chong-chen 7, 15, 20, 22–3, 51, 67, 89–107 • Chang Xueren (son of above) 107 • Chaplin, Charlie 63 • Charlotte, Princess 75 • Charroux, Robert 113 • Chiang Kai-shek, Madame (Song Meilin) 19, 101 • Chiao Cheng-chi, 'Arnold' 92 • Chopin, Frédéric 66 • Chouang Tsen 106 • 'Cinerama' 69 • Citroën 41 • *Cœurs Vaillants* 4, 7 • Colman, Ronald 69 • Conway, Jack 67 • Crabb, Lionel 'Buster' 56, 57

D Dalai Lama, the 105 • Dargaud, Georges 123 • D-Day landings 83 • Debruyne, Guy 39 • Debussy, Claude 66, 110 • de Chirico, Giorgio 35 • de Dudzeele, Marie-Helène, Countess 6 • de Gaulle, Charles, General 4, 93 • Degrelle, Léon 31, 53, 119 • Dehaye, Marcel 4, 122 • De Jaeger, Stefan 5 • Delaunay, Robert 33 • Delaunay, Sonia 5 • de Laurencin, Marie 40 • Delville, brothers 31, 78 • de Monfreid, Henri 45, 46 • De Moor, Bob 21, 124 • Dessicy, Guy 87, 109, 110, 115, 119 • Dessicy, Léona 110 • de Tirtoff, Romain (Erté) 79 • Devos, Alice 55 • Dickens, Charles 26, 27, 66 • Dierick, Charles 67, 69 • Dietrich, Marlene 93 • Disney, Walt 38, 113 • Donat, Robert 65 • Douglas, Kirk 60, 67 • Douillet, Joseph 52 • Dubuffet, Jean 5 • Dufour, Ninie 29

E *Eagle*, comic 4

F Fairbanks, Douglas, Snr 67 • Fanny (Rodwell; previously Remi; née Vlamynck) 5, 7, 9, 15–17, 19, 20, 36, 37, 40, 63, 65, 66, 69, 77, 83, 102, 105, 107, 114, 124, 125 • *Femmes d'Aujourd'hui* 36 • Flammarion, publisher 93 • Flavin, Dan 5, 37 • *Flying Scotsman*, locomotive 65 • Fontana, Lucio 5, 36, 40 • Ford, John 63 • Ford, Model T 60 • Forlani, Rémo 72 • Franco, Francisco, General 53 • Freud, Sigmund 66 • Furtwängler, Wilhelm 54 • Futurists, Italian 33, 110

G Gall, Father 17, 82, 83 • Gallimard, publisher 113 • Gauguin, Paul 34, 35 • Germaine (Remi; née Kieckens) 7, 17, 40, 44, 77, 83, 92, 93, 102, 122, 125 • George IV, King 75 • *Georges Philippar*, liner 45, 93 • Gish, Lilian 67 • Goscinny, René 73, 113 • Gosset, Father Léon 91, 92, 97 • Griffiths, David W. 67

H Hardy, Oliver 63 • Harlow, Jean 60 • Harmon, Larry 71 • *Harper's Bazaar*, magazine 79 • Herbin, Auguste 5 • Herget, H. M. 56 • Heuvelmans, Bernard 39 • Hitchcock, Alfred 25, 64, 65 • Hitler, Adolf 53, 101, 109, 119 • Hockney, David 5 • Hope, Anthony (Sir Anthony Hope Hawkins) 69 • Horta, Victor 27

I Ibañez, Blasco 93 • Ickx, Pierre 79 • Ingres, Jean Auguste Dominique 39 • International Settlement, Shanghai 19, 20, 61

J Jacobs, Edgar-Pierre 55, 98, 99, 121 • Jarrett, Keith 66 • John Paul II, Pope 9 • Jung, Carl G. 66, 102, 113

K Kandinsky, Vasily 33 • Kang-Hi, Hergé's Siamese cat 15 • Keaton, Buster 6, 63, 66 • Kenton, Erle C. 67 • Kessel, Joseph 45 • Keystone Kops 62, 63 • Khrushchev, Nikita 56 • Kupka, Frantisek 33

L *L'Actualité* 13 • *La Libre Belgique* 53 • Lang, Fritz 62 • Langdon, Harry 63 • Laughton, Charles 67 • Laurel, Stan 63 • Leblanc, Raymond 7, 55, 71, 79, 112, 115, 120, 121, 122, 123, 124 • *Le Boy-Scout Belge* 7, 30, 31, 43, 45, 59, 78 • *L'Écho Illustré* 4 • *Le Crapouillot* 63 • Léger, Fernand 34, 35 • Legros, Fernand 57, 69 • *Le Matin de Paris* 11 • Lemnitzer, Lyman, General 85 • *Le Monde* 30, 77 • Lennon, John 111 • Léopold of Saxe-Coburg (Léopold I of Belgium) 75 • Léopold II 6 • Léopold III

6, 117 • *Le Petit Vingtième* 7, 13, 14, 23, 30, 44, 46, 47, 48, 49, 52, 53, 55, 90, 91, 92, 109, 120, 121, 122 • *Le Quotidien de Paris* 11 • Lesieur, sunflower oil 41 • Lesne, Charles 13 • *Le Soir* 7, 11, 25, 27, 34, 49, 53, 55, 71, 115, 117, 118, 120, 121, 124 • *Le Soir Jeunesse* 7, 52, 53, 117, 118, 121 • *Le Vingtième Littéraire et Artistique* 44 • *Le Vingtième Siècle* 7, 12, 13, 30, 31, 43, 46, 49, 53, 56, 57, 78, 79, 117, 119, 120 • *Libération* 10, 11 • Lichtenstein, Roy 5, 19, 38, 39, 41, 71 • Lin, Richard 5 • Lin, 'Suzanne' 92 • Lindsay, John 18, 19 • Lloyd, Harold 63, 69 • Londres, Albert 45, 92, 93 • Lou, Tseng-tsieng (Father Pierre Célestin Lou) 92, 93 • Lumière, Auguste and Louis 59

M Mafeking, siege of 75 • Magritte, René 16 • Malevich, Kasimir 33, 34 • Malraux, André 92 • *Manchester Guardian* 46, 52 • Man Ray 43 • Mao Zedong 19 • Marco Polo 101, 106 • Marlborough Fine Art, London 5 • Matisse, Henri 38 • Ma Xiangbo 97, 98, 99, 100, 107 • Methuen, publisher 4, 73, 114 • Miró, Joan 5, 7, 36, 39 • Modigliani, Amedeo 34, 35 • Moholy-Nagy, Laszlo 40, 43 • Monet, Claude 19, 34, 35, 39 • Monroe, Marilyn 60 • Montand, Yves 65, 66 • Montgomery, Bernard, Field Marshal 120 • Moukden incident 95 • Movietone 61 • Muggeridge, Malcolm 46, 52 • Mussolini, Benito 44, 46, 53, 101, 109

N Neut, Father Edouard 92, 97 • Newman, Ronald 83 • Noland, Kenneth 5 • Nutella spread 41

O Onassis, Aristotle 35, 66 • *O Papagaio*, Portuguese children's periodical 4 • *Ordzhonikidze*, Soviet cruiser 56

P Pabst, Georg Wilhelm 63 • *Paris Match* 57 • Parke Bennet, auctioneer 35 • Pathé News 61, 67 • Peeters, Benoît 66 • Permeke, Constant 36 • Picasso, Pablo 33, 34, 35 • Pickford, Mary 60 • Pink Floyd 66, 110 • *Planète*, magazine 113 • Poliakoff, Serge 5, 35, 36, 39 • Pop Art 38, 110

R Rackham, Arthur 46 • Rank Organisation, films 67 • Rasmüssen, Tonning 37 • Rauschenberg, Robert 5 • Red Cloud, Sioux chief 19 • Regnier, Michel (Greg) 72, 73 • Reinhardt, Django 65 • Remi, Alexis (father) 7, 27, 63 • Remi, Denise (niece) 123 • Remi, Élisabeth (mother) 6, 7, 27 • Remi, Georges (nephew) 123 • Remi, Jeannot (sister-in-law) 123 • Remi, Léon (uncle) 7, 29, 63 • Remi, Paul (brother) 4, 6, 26, 27, 29, 123 • Renoir, Pierre 34, 35 • Ricklin, Dr Franz 102 • Robinson, Edward G. 66 • Rodin, Auguste 95 • Rombeaux, Égide, Professor 95 • Rothko, Mark 36, 100 • Rubens, Peter Paul 95

S Sadoul, Numa 71, 115 • Saint-Boniface Review 6 • St Francis Xavier 97 • Saint-Ogan, Alain 31 • Salik anoraks 41 • Satie, Erik 66 • Schubert, Franz 66, 110 • *Scoop*, novel 14, 46 • Sidney Janis Gallery, New York 5 • Sisley, Alfred 35 • Smits, Jakob 36 • Soupart, André 37 • Spielberg, Steven 6, 59, 69, 71, 73 • Stal, Marcel 5, 34, 36, 38, 39, 40 • Stella, Frank 5 • Sterckx, Pierre 39 • Studios Hergé 5, 7, 36, 38, 39, 41, 55, 56, 71, 73, 110, 123

T Tao Töking 106 • Taoism 20, 66, 95, 105 • Talbot, Jean-Pierre 72 • Tebaldi, Renata 66 • Thadée, Father 92 • *The National Geographic Magazine* 56 • *The Rainbow* 31 • *The Times Literary Supplement* 4 • *Tintin* magazine 7, 49, 55, 71, 72, 79, 112, 115, 120, 121, 122, 123 • Trenet, Charles 65

U Uderzo, Albert 73, 113

V Valentino, Rudolph 60, 67 • Valet, Gérard 106 • Van Cutsem, Marie-Louise (Milou) 7, 27, 29 • Van Eyck, Jan 95 • Van Geluwe, Hergé's tailor 39 • Van Lint, Louis 39 • Van Melkebeke, Jacques 34, 39, 40, 111, 121 • Van Puyvelde, Léo 39 • Van Ruisdael, Jacob 9 • Vasarely, Victor 5 • *Vendredi, Samedi, Dimanche* 11 • Vermeer, Jan 39 • Vincent, René 44 • von Perkhammer, Heinz 93 • von Sternberg, Josef 69, 93 • von Stroheim, Erich 27 • *Votre 'Vingtième' Madame* 43, 44

W Wallez, Father Norbert 7, 12, 13, 30, 43, 48, 49, 53, 122 • Warhol, Andy 5, 18, 19, 24, 25, 38, 41, 71, 110 • Waugh, Evelyn 14, 46 • Wei, Pierre 105 • Welles, Orson 69 • Wesselman, Tom 5 • Weverbergh, René 78 • White, Pearl 67 • Wilson, Georges 72 • Wilson, Lambert 72 • Wodehouse, P. G. 54 • Wong, Anna May 93

X Xueren, see Chang

Y Yates, Dornford (Major C. W. Mercer) 29 • Yeti, the 103, 105

Z Zen Buddhism 5, 36, 66, 95, 105 • 'Zen Coiffure' 5

Copyright acknowledgements:

Page 37
• Serge Poliakoff © SABAM Belgium 2007
• *Caboda Roca*, 1982, by Tonning Rasmüssen © SABAM Belgium 2007
• Lucio Fontana © All rights reserved
Page 38
• Portrait of Hergé, 1977, by Andy Warhol © Andy Warhol / J. P. Stercq
Page 39
• *Rouen Cathedral*, 1969, by Roy Lichtenstein © SABAM Belgium 2007

Cover and dust jacket
Front © Archives Studios Hergé
Back © Kayaert